Budgeting Basics for Beginners

Author

Danielle A Calise

Copyright © [2024] by [Stylin' Spirit]

All rights reserved. No part of this book may be reproduced or transmitted in any form or by any means, electronic or mechanical, including photocopying, recording, or by any information storage and retrieval system, without prior written permission from the author, except for the inclusion of brief quotations in a review.

Published by [Stylin' Spirit]

www.stylin-spirit.com

First Edition: April 2024

Table of Contents

Introduction to Budgeting Basics 5

Master Brainstorming List for Budget Planning . 11

Housing Costs 19

Transportation Expenses 25

Budgeting for Groceries and Household Supplies 31

Understanding the Importance of Employment-Related Expenses 39

Health and Medical Expenses 47

Nurturing Care for Dependents 53

Pet Care 61

Establishing Meaningful Traditions 67

Socializing Expenses 85

Analyzing Debt Obligations 107

Importance of Insurance in Financial Planning 113

Introduction to Investing and Retirement Planning 121

Identification and Categorization of Miscellaneous Expenses 133

Recap of Key Points on Investing and Retirement 139

Financial Planning and Wealth Management Strategies 153

Budget Planning List 159

Introduction to Budgeting Basics

Budget planning is a fundamental aspect of financial management that is the cornerstone of a successful financial future. By carefully assessing your income sources and expenses, creating a comprehensive budget plan can help you gain control over your financial situation and achieve your long-term financial goals.

One of the key components of budget planning is understanding the importance of setting financial boundaries and priorities. By establishing a budget, you can allocate your resources effectively to cover essential expenses, save for the future, and even indulge in occasional splurges without jeopardizing your financial stability. This proactive approach enables you to make informed financial decisions and provides a roadmap for achieving financial security.

Moreover, budget planning involves identifying your financial goals and aligning your spending habits with these objectives. Whether you aim to build an emergency fund, save for a major purchase, or invest for retirement, creating a budget allows you to track your progress toward these goals and make necessary adjustments. By fostering a proactive mindset and instilling discipline in your financial habits, budget planning empowers you to take charge of your financial well-being and work towards a brighter financial future.

In the following sections, we will delve deeper into the process of generating ideas for budgeting, helping you identify your income sources, track your spending patterns, and align your financial priorities to create a comprehensive budget plan that reflects your financial aspirations. With a solid foundation in budget planning, you can pave the way for financial success and build a secure financial future for yourself and your loved ones.

Generating Ideas for Budgeting

Generating budgeting ideas is a crucial step in budget planning that lays the foundation for a successful financial strategy. This phase involves a deep dive into your financial landscape, encompassing income sources, expenses, spending habits, and long-term financial goals.

The first step in generating ideas for budgeting is to identify and catalog all sources of income. This includes not only your primary source of income, such as salary or wages, but also any additional sources like bonuses, freelance work, or passive income streams. By clearly understanding all inflows, you can accurately assess your financial capacity for budgeting.

Next, it is essential to meticulously track your spending patterns over a defined period, such as a month or quarter. This exercise categorizes expenses into different segments: housing, transportation, groceries, entertainment, and savings. By scrutinizing your spending habits, you can pinpoint areas where you may be overspending or identify opportunities for cost-cutting.

In tandem with tracking expenses, evaluating your financial goals and priorities is imperative. This entails determining short-term objectives, such as paying off debt or saving for a vacation, and long-term goals, like buying a home or retiring comfortably. Aligning your budget with your goals ensures that your financial resources are allocated optimally to support your aspirations.

Generating budgeting ideas involves delving into the intricacies of income sources, expenses, spending behaviors, and financial goals. This equips you with a comprehensive understanding of your financial landscape. This foundational knowledge serves as a springboard for developing a robust and effective budget plan that aligns with your aspirations and paves the way for financial prosperity.

Developing a Comprehensive Budget Plan

Now that you have generated ideas and insights by brainstorming and identifying your income sources and expenses, it is time to translate them into a concrete budget plan. A comprehensive budget plan is essential for effective financial management and achieving your financial goals. Here are the key steps to develop a comprehensive budget plan:

1. Organizing and Categorizing Expenses: Begin by categorizing your expenses into different groups, such as housing, transportation, groceries, utilities, entertainment, savings, and debt payments. This organization will help you see where your money is going and

identify areas where you can potentially cut back or reallocate funds.

2. Creating Realistic Budget Targets: Set specific and achievable targets for each expense category based on your income and financial priorities. Be realistic about your spending habits and factor in any irregular or unexpected expenses that may arise. Setting realistic targets will help you stay on track with your budget and make adjustments as needed.

3. Implementing Strategies for Successful Budget Management: Develop strategies to track your expenses, monitor your progress, and make adjustments as necessary. Use budgeting tools and apps to streamline the process and stay organized. Regularly review your budget plan to ensure you remain within your set limits and adjust as needed to meet your financial goals.

By developing a comprehensive budget plan that is well-organized, realistic, and actively managed, you will pave the way for financial stability, control over your finances, and progress toward achieving your short and long-term financial objectives. Remember, a budget is not meant to restrict you but to empower you to make informed financial decisions and achieve economic success.

Master Brainstorming List for Budget Planning

Overview of Housing Costs in Budget Planning

Understanding and effectively managing housing costs is crucial for financial stability and security in budget planning. Housing expenses typically comprise a significant portion of an individual or family's budget, making it essential to evaluate and plan for these expenses carefully.

Housing costs encompass various elements, including rent or mortgage payments, utilities, maintenance costs, insurance, and property taxes. By breaking down these expenses and analyzing them as part of the overall budget, individuals can better understand their financial obligations related to housing.

Rent or mortgage payments are usually the most substantial housing costs for individuals. Renters must budget for monthly rent payments, while homeowners need to consider mortgage principal and interest payments. Understanding the terms of the lease or mortgage agreement is essential to assessing these costs and planning for them appropriately and accurately.

Utilities such as electricity, water, gas, and internet services are ongoing expenses that must also be factored into the housing budget. Individuals should track their utility usage and explore ways to conserve energy to reduce these costs wherever possible.

Maintenance costs are another critical aspect of housing expenses. Homeowners, in particular, need to budget for their property's repairs, maintenance, and upkeep. Planning for routine maintenance tasks and setting aside funds for unexpected repairs can help prevent financial strain in the long run.

Insurance and property taxes are additional components of housing costs that individuals should consider in their budget planning. Homeowners must have adequate homeowners' insurance to protect their property and belongings in case of unforeseen events such as natural disasters or accidents. Property taxes vary depending on the location and value of the property and can significantly impact the overall housing budget.

A comprehensive understanding of housing costs is essential for effective budget planning. By taking the time to calculate and manage these expenses, individuals can better control their finances, avoid financial strain, and work towards their long-term financial goals.

Calculating and Managing Housing Expenses

When budgeting for housing, it is crucial to understand its various expenses clearly. From rent or mortgage payments to utilities and maintenance costs, managing housing expenses requires careful planning and consideration.

1. Rent or Mortgage Payments: Most of your housing expenses will likely be rent or mortgage payments. Setting a budget that aligns with your income and financial goals is essential. Consider the monthly payment and additional costs, such as homeowner association fees or property taxes, when calculating this expense.

2. Utilities and Maintenance Costs: Besides your rent or mortgage, you must budget for utilities such as electricity, water, gas, and internet. These expenses can vary based on your usage and location, so

tracking and monitoring them regularly is essential. Maintenance costs, including repairs and upkeep, should also be factored into your housing budget to avoid unexpected financial burdens.

3. Insurance and Property Taxes: Insurance and property taxes are often overlooked housing expenses that can significantly impact your budget. Homeowner's insurance covers your property in case of damage or loss, while property taxes contribute to local infrastructure and services. Understanding these costs and ensuring they are included in your budget will help you manage your overall housing expenses effectively.

By accurately calculating and managing your housing expenses, you can create a solid financial foundation and achieve greater stability in your budgeting efforts. Through careful planning and mindful spending, you can ensure that your housing costs align with your financial goals and contribute to your overall financial well-being.

Strategies for Budgeting and Saving on Housing Costs

To effectively budget and save on housing costs, it is essential to implement strategic financial planning and smart decision-making. Here are some proven strategies to help you manage your housing expenses efficiently:

1. Conduct a thorough review of your current housing situation: Analyze your current housing expenses and identify areas where you can cut costs. Look for opportunities to reduce utility bills, renegotiate rent or mortgage rates, or explore alternative housing options that might be more cost-effective.

2. Set realistic housing budget goals: Establishing a clear and achievable budget for your housing expenses is crucial. Consider your income, other financial obligations, and savings goals when determining how much you can afford to allocate toward housing costs. Setting realistic budget limits will help you avoid financial strain and ensure long-term affordability.

3. Explore cost-saving measures: Look for ways to reduce your housing expenses without sacrificing quality of life. Consider energy-efficient upgrades to your home, such as installing programmable thermostats or energy-saving appliances, that can help lower utility bills over time. Additionally, explore options like refinancing your mortgage or downsizing to a more affordable living space to save on housing costs.

4. Utilize available resources and assistance programs: Take advantage of government programs, housing subsidies, or financial assistance initiatives that may be available to help lower your housing expenses. Research affordable housing options in your area, explore property tax relief programs or seek out rental assistance programs to alleviate financial burdens related to housing costs.

5. Prioritize saving for emergencies and future housing needs: Building a robust emergency fund is essential to protecting yourself from unexpected housing-related expenses, such as repairs or

maintenance issues. Additionally, consider setting aside funds in a dedicated savings account or investment vehicle to save for long-term housing goals, such as homeownership or retirement housing.

By implementing these strategies and maintaining a proactive approach to managing your housing expenses, you can make informed financial decisions and optimize your budgeting efforts to save on housing costs effectively.

Housing Costs

Assessing the Condition of Your Home: Maintaining a safe and functional living environment requires a proactive approach to assessing the condition of your home. Regular inspections and maintenance checks are essential to identifying potential issues early on and prioritizing necessary repairs. Investing time and effort in this initial step can prevent small problems from escalating into costly emergencies.

Start by thoroughly inspecting your home, both inside and out. Pay attention to areas prone to wear and tear, such as roofs, gutters, windows, and HVAC systems. Look for signs of water damage, pest infestations, or structural issues that may compromise the integrity of your home. These observations will help you create a comprehensive maintenance plan tailored to your specific needs.

As you assess the condition of your home, consider the age and maintenance history of key components such as appliances, plumbing, and electrical systems. Keep track of when these systems were last serviced or upgraded to anticipate future maintenance requirements. Prioritize your maintenance tasks based on urgency and allocate resources accordingly to address potential risks and ensure the longevity of your home.

In addition to visual inspections, tools such as moisture meters, thermographic cameras, and radon detectors are utilized to detect hidden issues that may not be visible to the naked eye. Engaging professionals for specialized assessments, such as HVAC maintenance or termite inspections, can provide valuable insights and recommendations for maintaining your home in optimal condition.

Remember that regular maintenance is not just about fixing problems as they arise but also about taking a proactive approach to preserve the value and safety of your home. By staying attentive to the condition of your living space and addressing maintenance needs promptly, you can enhance your home's longevity and create a comfortable and secure environment for you and your loved ones.

Budgeting for Home Maintenance

When it comes to maintaining your home, budgeting is crucial in ensuring that your property remains in good condition while staying within your financial means. Setting aside funds for home maintenance is an essential aspect of responsible homeownership. Here are some key considerations for budgeting effectively for home maintenance:

1. Estimating Maintenance Costs: Start by assessing the current condition of your home and identifying any areas that require attention. Make a list of routine maintenance tasks such as HVAC system servicing, gutter cleaning, and lawn care. Research the typical costs of these tasks and factor them into your budget.

2. Planning for Repairs and Emergencies: Setting aside funds for unexpected repairs and emergencies is important besides routine maintenance. Major repairs such as roof leaks, plumbing issues, or appliance breakdowns can happen suddenly and require immediate attention. Having a contingency fund designated explicitly for home repairs can

help alleviate the financial burden when these situations arise.

3. Prioritizing Maintenance Projects: Not all home maintenance tasks are equal. Some projects may require immediate attention to prevent further damage, while others can be deferred later. Prioritize maintenance projects based on their urgency and their impact on your home's overall condition. Allocate your budget accordingly to address the most critical issues first.

4. Seeking Professional Advice: When budgeting for home maintenance, it is important to consult with professionals as needed. Contractors, home inspectors, and other experts can provide valuable insights into the condition of your home and recommend necessary maintenance or repairs. Consider obtaining multiple quotes for major projects to ensure you get the best value for your money.

By establishing a comprehensive budget for home maintenance and adhering to it diligently, you can protect your investment and safeguard the long-term value of your property. Remember that preventive maintenance is key to avoiding costly repairs down the line, so prioritize regular upkeep of your home to keep it in optimal condition.

DIY vs. Contracting Out

When it comes to maintaining your home, one of the decisions you'll frequently face is whether to handle tasks yourself or enlist the help of a professional service. Both options have pros and cons, and understanding when to DIY and when to hire a professional can save you time and money and ensure the job is done correctly.

DIY projects can be a fulfilling and cost-effective way to tackle minor home maintenance tasks. If you have the skills, tools, and time to complete a project, doing it yourself can save you money on labor costs. Additionally, DIY projects allow you to take pride in your home and learn new skills. However, it's important to recognize your limitations and know when a project is beyond your expertise.

On the other hand, hiring a professional service can offer expertise, efficiency, and peace of mind. Professionals bring experience and specialized tools to the job, ensuring it is done correctly and efficiently. They can also provide warranties or guarantees on their work, giving you added security. It is often best to leave it to the experts when dealing with complex or dangerous tasks, such as electrical work or structural repairs.

When deciding between DIY and professional services, consider the complexity of the task, your skill level, the time required, and the potential risks involved. It may be helpful to weigh the cost of DIY against hiring a professional, factoring in the value of your time and the potential for mistakes. Ultimately, the goal is to maintain your home safely and efficiently while staying within your budget and comfort level.

By understanding the advantages and limitations of DIY and professional services, you can make informed decisions that benefit your home and wallet. Whether you roll up your sleeves or call in the experts, prioritizing proper maintenance will ensure your home remains a safe and comfortable haven for years.

Transportation Expenses

Transportation expenses are vital to our daily lives, significantly impacting our ability to travel to work, run errands, and maintain our overall mobility. When considering our budget, we must account for the costs of owning and operating a vehicle.

One key component of transportation expenses is vehicle ownership costs. These costs encompass various factors contributing to the overall expenses of owning a car. Some of the primary ownership costs include insurance premiums, registration fees, regular maintenance, and unexpected repairs. It is crucial to factor in these expenses when creating a budget to ensure that you are adequately prepared to cover the costs associated with vehicle ownership.

Insurance is a mandatory expense that all vehicle owners must budget for. The cost of insurance premiums can vary depending on factors such as the type of coverage, your driving record, and the make and model of your vehicle. It is essential to shop around for insurance quotes to find the best coverage at an affordable price.

Registration fees are another ownership cost that should be considered. These fees are typically due annually and cover registering your vehicle with the state. Additionally, regular maintenance, such as oil changes, tire rotations, and brake inspections, are necessary to keep your vehicle running smoothly and prevent costly repairs down the line.

In addition to these recurring ownership costs, it is essential to budget for unexpected repairs that may arise. Setting aside a fund for vehicle repairs can provide peace of mind and ensure you are financially prepared for unforeseen maintenance needs.

By understanding and budgeting for the ownership costs associated with your vehicle, you can better manage your transportation expenses and ensure you have the financial resources necessary to maintain and operate your vehicle effectively.

Calculating Vehicle Ownership Costs

Calculating Vehicle Ownership Costs:

Understanding and calculating vehicle ownership costs is crucial to managing your finances effectively. Owning a vehicle involves more expenses than just the initial purchase price. To ensure you are prepared for these ongoing costs, breaking down and estimating the various components contributing to vehicle ownership expenses is essential.

One primary expense to consider is insurance. Auto insurance premiums vary based on your driving record, vehicle type, and location. By obtaining quotes from multiple insurance providers and comparing coverage options, you can find a policy that suits your needs while staying within your budget.

Registration and licensing fees are another aspect of vehicle ownership costs that must be factored in. These fees are typically paid annually and vary depending on the state or country in which you reside. Researching the specific requirements in your area is essential to accurately budgeting for these expenses.

Regular maintenance is crucial for keeping your vehicle in optimal condition and preventing costly repairs down the road. Budgeting for routine maintenance tasks such as oil changes, tire rotations, and brake inspections can help you avoid unexpected expenses and prolong the life of your vehicle.

In addition to routine maintenance, you should also set aside funds for unexpected repairs and emergencies. Cars can break down unexpectedly, and having a financial cushion for unexpected repair costs can provide peace of mind and prevent financial strain.

Depreciation is another cost associated with vehicle ownership that is often overlooked. As vehicles age, their value decreases, impacting their resale or trade-in value. Understanding your vehicle's depreciation rate can help you estimate its future value and make informed decisions about purchasing or selling your current vehicle.

By carefully calculating your vehicle ownership costs and including them in your budget, you can proactively manage your finances and avoid being caught off guard by unexpected expenses. Prioritizing regular maintenance, researching insurance options, and planning for depreciation can help you maintain financial stability while enjoying the convenience and mobility of owning a vehicle.

Managing Daily Transportation Costs

In managing daily transportation costs, it is essential to consider all the various expenses that can accumulate over time. From fuel and public transportation fees to parking and tolls, these costs can quickly add up and impact your overall budget.

Evaluating your transportation needs is crucial to efficiently managing your daily transportation expenses. Consider alternative modes of transportation, such as carpooling, biking, or utilizing public transportation, to reduce fuel costs and minimize wear and tear on your vehicle.

Planning your routes can also help you save money on fuel and reduce unnecessary mileage. Opt for the most direct and efficient routes to your destinations to lower fuel consumption and save time.

Another important aspect of managing daily transportation costs is taking advantage of discounts or promotions. Look for carpooling programs, public transportation passes, or loyalty programs that can help you save money on your daily commutes.

Furthermore, practicing eco-friendly driving habits, such as maintaining a steady speed, avoiding rapid acceleration and braking, and keeping your vehicle well-maintained, can improve fuel efficiency and lower overall transportation costs.

Finally, setting a transportation budget and regularly tracking your expenses can help you monitor your expenditures and identify areas for cost savings. By being mindful of your daily transportation expenses and implementing cost-saving strategies, you can effectively manage your budget and make informed decisions about your transportation needs.

Budgeting for Groceries and Household Supplies

When managing your household budget effectively, one key area to pay close attention to is your grocery and household supplies expenses. These items are essential for maintaining your home and ensuring that you and your family have what you need to live comfortably. However, these expenses can easily add up if not managed carefully. In this section, we will explore strategies for budgeting wisely for groceries and household supplies, helping you save money without compromising on quality.

Importance of Managing Grocery and Household Expenses Effective budgeting for groceries and household supplies is crucial for maintaining financial stability and achieving financial goals. By setting a budget and sticking to it, you can avoid overspending and ensure that your money is allocated efficiently. This helps you save money in the long run and promotes responsible spending habits.

Setting Realistic Budget Goals To start, assessing your current spending habits on groceries and household supplies is essential. Look at your past expenses in these categories to determine an average monthly spending amount. Set realistic budget goals based on your income and financial obligations. Consider factors such as your household size, dietary preferences, and any special needs that may affect your grocery expenses.

Strategies for Saving Money on Groceries and Household Supplies You can implement several strategies to save money on your grocery and household supply expenses. One effective method is meal planning, which involves mapping out your meals for the week and creating a shopping list based on those recipes. This helps you avoid impulse purchases and reduces the likelihood of food waste.

Additionally, take advantage of coupons, promotions, and discounts from supermarkets and online retailers. By being mindful of sales and special offers, you can stock up on essential items at a lower cost. Consider joining loyalty programs or using cashback apps to maximize your savings on groceries and household supplies.

Comparison shopping and bulk buying are other effective strategies for saving money on essential items. Before purchasing, compare prices at different stores to ensure you get the best deal. Buying in bulk can also result in significant savings, especially for non-perishable items or products you use frequently.

By incorporating these budgeting techniques and money-saving strategies into your grocery and household supply shopping routine, you can effectively manage your expenses while meeting your household needs. With careful planning and mindful spending, you can achieve financial stability and peace of mind in your day-to-day expenses.

Smart Shopping Tips

Develop smart shopping habits to manage your grocery and household supplies budget effectively. By incorporating strategic techniques and mindful practices into your shopping routine, you can maximize savings and make the most of your allocated funds.

Meal planning and food preparation are pivotal aspects of smart shopping. Creating weekly or monthly meal plans can streamline your grocery shopping list and minimize impulse purchases. Planning your meals also allows you to take advantage of sales and discounts on essential items, helping you save money in the long run.

Utilizing coupons and discounts is another key strategy in smart shopping. Look for promotional offers, digital coupons, and loyalty programs at your preferred grocery stores. You can capitalize on additional savings and lower overall grocery costs by clipping coupons, downloading mobile apps, or signing up for rewards programs.

Comparison shopping and bulk buying are effective ways to stretch your budget when purchasing household supplies. Before purchasing, compare prices across different retailers to ensure you get the best deal. Consider buying items in bulk or larger quantities for products you use regularly, as this can be more cost-effective in the long term.

By implementing these smart shopping tips into your routine, you can optimize your grocery and household supply budget, making the most of every dollar spent while meeting your family's needs.

Organizing Household Supplies

Efficient management of household supplies is essential for maintaining a well-organized and functional home. By implementing strategic organization tactics, you can streamline household operations, save time, and minimize waste. Here are some effective strategies to help you optimize your household supplies:

1. Inventory Management: Tracking your household supplies inventory is crucial for preventing unnecessary purchases and ensuring you always have what you need. Create a system for tracking your supplies—a physical inventory list or a digital spreadsheet. Regularly update this list to reflect your current stock levels and avoid overstocking or running out of essential items.

2. Efficient Storage Solutions: Invest in storage solutions that maximize space and make it easy to access and organize household supplies. Utilize storage

containers, bins, shelves, and labeling systems to categorize and store items in a functional and visually appealing way. Consider utilizing space-saving organizers, such as over-the-door racks or under-shelf baskets, to make the most of every inch of storage space available in your home.

3. Minimizing Waste and Maximizing Usage: To reduce waste and save money, strive to use your household supplies efficiently. Monitor expiration dates on perishable items and rotate stock to ensure nothing goes to waste. Implement a "first in, first out" system for organizing your pantry and other supplies to prevent items from expiring before you can use them. Additionally, consider repurposing or upcycling household items no longer needed to extend their usefulness and minimize waste.

By implementing these organizational strategies, you can create a well-managed and efficient household supply system that supports your daily activities and promotes a clutter-free, functional living space. Prioritize organization and efficiency in managing your household supplies to enhance your home's overall functionality and enjoyment.

Understanding the Importance of Employment-Related Expenses

In today's dynamic and fast-paced work environment, it is essential to recognize the significance of employment-related expenses in maintaining financial stability and achieving long-term financial goals. Employment expenses encompass many costs that employees often incur in their professional endeavors. From work attire to commuting expenses and professional development opportunities to technology investments, these expenses play a crucial role in supporting individuals in their career pursuits and maximizing their potential in the workforce.

One key reason for understanding and budgeting for employment-related expenses is to ensure that individuals are adequately prepared to meet the demands of their job roles. By planning and allocating resources to these expenses, employees can equip themselves with the necessary tools and resources to perform their duties effectively and excel in their respective fields. Moreover, by estimating and accounting for these costs in their overall budget, individuals can avoid financial strain and surprises arising from job-related expenditures.

Another critical aspect of recognizing the importance of employment-related expenses is their impact on an individual's financial well-being and prospects. By prudently managing these expenses and integrating them into a comprehensive budget plan, individuals can balance meeting their job requirements and pursuing their long-term financial objectives. This includes saving for retirement, investing in personal development, and building a solid financial foundation that supports their lifestyle and aspirations.

Furthermore, understanding the significance of employment-related expenses can also lead to improved financial awareness and discipline. By recognizing the various components of these expenses and their necessity in the professional realm, individuals can make informed decisions about their spending habits and prioritize their financial commitments accordingly. This heightened awareness can empower individuals to make strategic choices that align with their goals and values, ultimately fostering a sense of financial independence and security.

The importance of employment-related expenses cannot be understated in today's complex and evolving work environment. By acknowledging the essential role these costs play in supporting individuals in their careers and financial journey, individuals can proactively manage and budget for these expenses to achieve greater financial stability and success in the long run. Ultimately, understanding and prioritizing employment-related expenses is key to unlocking the full potential of one's professional endeavors and building a solid foundation for a prosperous future.

Key Components of Employment-Related Expenses

In today's dynamic and competitive work environment, individuals must understand and fully manage the various components of employment-related expenses. These expenses encompass various categories directly impacting our professional lives and financial well-being.

One key component of employment-related expenses is work attire. Whether it's business professional attire for board meetings or specialized uniforms for specific job roles, the cost of maintaining a professional appearance can add up quickly. It is important to allocate a portion of your budget towards clothing and grooming items to ensure you always present yourself in a polished and professional manner.

Commuting costs form another significant aspect of employment-related expenses. Whether you rely on public transportation, drive your vehicle, or utilize ride-sharing services, the costs of getting to and from work can be substantial. When budgeting, it is crucial to factor in these costs, as they are a recurring and necessary part of your job responsibilities.

Professional development is an essential component of any successful career. Investing in workshops, courses, conferences, and certifications can help you stay current in your field and advance your professional skills. While these opportunities may come with a price tag, the long-term benefits of investing in your professional growth far outweigh the initial costs.

In today's digital age, technology expenses are becoming increasingly important. Technology costs are crucial to employment-related expenses, from purchasing a new laptop for remote work to subscribing to software tools for project management. Evaluating which technology investments are necessary for your job and allocating a budget to ensure you have the tools needed to perform effectively is vital.

Understanding the key components of employment-related expenses is essential for maintaining financial stability and advancing your career. By carefully managing work attire, commuting costs, professional development, and technology expenses, you can effectively navigate the financial aspects of your job and achieve your long-term financial goals.

Balancing Work-Related Costs with Financial Goals

In today's fast-paced work environment, it is crucial to balance meeting job-related expenses and working towards your financial aspirations. Effectively managing employment-related costs is about keeping up with the demands of your job and aligning these expenses with your long-term financial objectives.

One key strategy for achieving this balance is incorporating job-related expenses into your budget plan. By including these costs as a separate category in your budget, you can track and monitor how much you spend on work-related items each month. This will give you a clear picture of how these expenses impact your financial situation.

It is important to prioritize your financial goals when considering work-related costs. Assess the necessity of each expense and determine whether it is helping you progress towards your financial targets or merely a convenience. By evaluating the value that each job-related expense adds to your career advancement or job satisfaction, you can make informed decisions about where to allocate your resources.

Striking a balance between work-related costs and financial goals also involves being mindful of your spending patterns. Look for opportunities to optimize expenses by finding cost-effective alternatives or negotiating better deals. This could include carpooling to reduce commuting costs, taking advantage of employer-sponsored benefits, or investing in professional development opportunities with a clear return on investment.

Ultimately, aligning your work-related costs with your financial objectives can ensure that you make purposeful decisions supporting your long-term financial well-being. Prioritizing your financial goals, tracking your expenses, and optimizing your spending will help you manage your job-related costs effectively and set you on a path toward achieving financial success.

Health and Medical Expenses

Personal Grooming and Hygiene:

Personal grooming and hygiene are essential aspects of self-care that contribute to our overall well-being and confidence. Taking care of our physical appearance enhances our external image and boosts our self-esteem and mental health. This section will explore the importance of maintaining good grooming habits while staying within budget constraints.

Investing in basic hygiene products is non-negotiable when it comes to personal grooming. Items such as soap, shampoo, toothpaste, and deodorant are essential for daily cleanliness and should be included in your budget as recurring expenses. While it may be tempting to splurge on luxury brands, plenty of budget-friendly options offer quality and effectiveness.

Additionally, consider incorporating DIY grooming practices into your routine to save money without compromising on self-care. For example, making your own face masks or hair treatments using natural ingredients can be a cost-effective way to pamper yourself at home.

This budget-friendly approach allows you to customize products based on your specific skin or hair care needs.

Maintaining a personal care routine within budget constraints requires thoughtful planning and prioritization. Identify your must-have grooming products and allocate a portion of your budget to cover these essentials. Consider shopping during sales or using coupons to further capitalize on discounts and stretch your grooming budget. Remember, self-care is an investment in yourself, and finding a balance between quality grooming practices and financial responsibility is key to achieving both physical well-being and financial stability.

Health and Wellness:

In the realm of health and wellness, it is essential to prioritize both physical and mental well-being within the constraints of your budget. Maintaining good health is crucial for your overall quality of life and plays a significant role in your financial stability in the long run.

Budgeting for healthcare expenses should be a top priority. This includes allocating funds for insurance premiums, co-pays, and any out-of-pocket costs that may arise. By planning for these expenses in advance, you can avoid financial strain when faced with unexpected medical bills.

Furthermore, investing in preventive care can help you avoid potential health issues and reduce the likelihood of costly treatments. Regular check-ups, screenings, and vaccinations are all pillars of a proactive approach to health that can save you money in the long term.

In addition to medical care, wellness activities should be factored into your budget. Whether it's a gym membership, fitness classes, or wellness retreats, allocating funds for activities that nourish your body and mind is an investment in your overall well-being.

Maintaining a balanced approach to health and wellness within your budget is about making strategic choices that align with your priorities. By proactively managing your healthcare expenses and incorporating wellness practices into your lifestyle, you can safeguard both your physical and financial health for the future.

Beauty and Self-Care:

In pursuing overall well-being, it is essential to recognize the significance of self-care practices contributing to our physical, mental, and emotional health. Beauty and self-care routines are not merely about aesthetics; they are about nurturing ourselves and enhancing our self-worth.

In beauty and self-care, balancing indulging in treatments and products that make us feel good and maintaining financial responsibility is crucial. While there is no denying the allure of luxurious beauty products and treatments, numerous cost-effective ways exist to prioritize self-care without breaking the bank.

One approach to integrating beauty and self-care into your budget is prioritizing essentials and investing in high-quality products that offer long-lasting benefits. Consider identifying key skincare products tailored to your skin type and concerns, as a well-curated skincare routine can provide tangible benefits for your skin's health.

Additionally, exploring DIY beauty hacks can be a fun and budget-friendly way to pamper yourself. From creating homemade face masks with natural ingredients to mastering the art of at-home manicures, there are plenty of creative ways to indulge in self-care without overspending.

It is also essential to recognize that self-care extends beyond external beauty rituals. Engaging in activities that promote relaxation and mental well-being, such as meditation, yoga, or journaling, can be just as crucial for maintaining a holistic sense of self-care.

Ultimately, the key to incorporating beauty and self-care practices into your budget is to approach it with intentionality and mindfulness. By prioritizing self-care within your financial planning and exploring affordable alternatives, you can cultivate a routine that nurtures your physical appearance and inner well-being.

Nurturing Care for Dependents

Nurturing Care for Dependents is crucial to a responsible individual's life. It ensures the safety, well-being, and development of children and dependents. Providing a safe and nurturing environment for dependents is paramount, as it lays the foundation for their overall growth and success in life.

Meeting children's and dependents' physical and emotional needs involves providing food, shelter, and clothing and offering love, support, and guidance. Creating a positive and nurturing atmosphere where dependents feel comfortable expressing themselves and seeking help when needed is essential.

Building strong relationships and bonds with dependents is vital for their emotional and psychological development. Spending quality time with children and dependents, engaging in activities, and having meaningful conversations help strengthen the bond and create lasting memories.

Financial Responsibilities towards dependents are significant and require careful planning and budgeting. Ensuring that dependents' needs and expenses are met, including education and extra-curricular activities, is essential for their growth and development. Planning for future financial security, such as saving for their education or setting up a trust fund, can provide peace of mind and stability for dependents in the long run.

Nurturing Care for Dependents encompasses creating a safe and loving environment, meeting their physical and emotional needs, building strong relationships, and fulfilling financial responsibilities. By prioritizing the well-being and development of dependents, individuals can contribute to their growth and success, laying a solid foundation for a bright future.

Financial Responsibilities:

In fulfilling our financial responsibilities towards our dependents, it is crucial to approach this task with careful planning and foresight. Budgeting for the needs and expenses of our loved ones requires a structured and disciplined approach. We must prioritize essential expenses such as housing, food, education, and healthcare for our dependents.

Education is a key aspect of our financial responsibilities towards children. Providing access to quality education and supporting their extra-curricular activities significantly affect their overall development. Planning for the costs associated with education, such as tuition fees, books, and school supplies, should be factored into our budgeting process.

Additionally, ensuring the future financial security of our dependents is a fundamental component of our financial responsibilities. This includes setting aside funds for their future endeavors, such as college education or vocational training. Investing in savings accounts or education funds can help secure their financial future and provide them with opportunities for growth and success.

In managing our financial responsibilities towards our dependents, it is essential to maintain open communication and transparency regarding financial matters. Teaching them about financial literacy and responsibility from a young age can empower them to make informed decisions and develop good money management habits for the future.

Ultimately, fulfilling our financial responsibilities towards our dependents is a testament to our commitment to their well-being and future success. By approaching this task with diligence and care, we can ensure our loved ones are provided for and supported in all aspects of their lives.

Health and Wellness:

Prioritizing health and wellness is essential for ensuring the well-being of our dependents. Promoting healthy habits and lifestyle choices for our children and loved ones is crucial to caregiving. We can contribute to their physical and mental well-being by instilling good practices and fostering a supportive environment.

Regular physical activity is vital for developing strong bodies and minds. Whether through organized sports, recreational activities, or simply playing outdoors, staying active helps maintain a healthy weight, promotes cardiovascular health, and enhances mood and cognitive function. Setting aside time for physical exercise benefits our dependents' physical health and instills discipline and a sense of accomplishment.

In addition to physical activity, nutrition is fundamental to maintaining good health. A balanced and nutritious diet of fruits, vegetables, whole grains, and lean proteins fuels our dependents' bodies with essential nutrients and energy. Teaching them the importance of healthy food choices and developing positive eating habits sets the foundation for a lifetime of wellness.

Furthermore, ensuring that our dependents have access to regular medical check-ups and preventive healthcare services is crucial for early detection and management of potential health issues. Regular visits to healthcare providers, vaccinations, and screenings help monitor their growth and development, prevent illness, and promote overall well-being.

By promoting healthy habits and lifestyle choices for our dependents, we nurture their physical health and support their emotional and mental welfare. Encouraging open communication, active listening, and providing a safe space for expression are essential to fostering positive mental health and emotional well-being.

By prioritizing health and wellness in the care of our dependents, we are investing in their long-term happiness and success. Our guidance and support help them develop the tools and habits to lead healthy and fulfilling lives.

- Promoting Healthy Habits and Lifestyle Choices for Dependents.

  Promoting healthy habits and lifestyle choices for dependents is crucial to providing proper care and ensuring their long-term well-being. As a responsible caregiver, it is important to instill healthy habits early to set a strong foundation for a healthy lifestyle.

One key way to promote healthy habits is by leading by example. Children often emulate the behaviors of the adults around them, so it is essential to prioritize your health and well-being. By demonstrating healthy habits such as eating nutritious meals, staying active, and managing stress effectively, you can positively influence the habits of your dependents.

Encouraging physical activity is another important aspect of promoting a healthy lifestyle for dependents. Regular exercise helps children develop strong muscles and bones and improves their overall mood and mental well-being. Whether engaging in sports, going for family walks, or participating in active playtime, finding fun ways to incorporate physical activity into your dependents' daily routine is key.

It is also crucial to teach dependents about the importance of a balanced diet and healthy food choices. Providing nutritious meals and snacks, involving them in meal planning and preparation, and educating them about the benefits of eating various foods can help instill lifelong healthy eating habits.

Limiting screen time and promoting positive social interactions are also important factors in promoting a healthy lifestyle for dependents. Encouraging less time in front of screens and more time engaging in outdoor activities, hobbies, and social interactions can help foster physical, mental, and emotional well-being.

Promoting healthy habits and lifestyle choices for dependents requires a proactive approach focusing on modeling healthy behavior, encouraging physical activity, prioritizing nutritious eating habits, and fostering positive social interactions. Investing in the health and well-being of your dependents sets them up for a lifetime of good health and happiness.

Pet Care

Discuss the importance of pet care in maintaining the health and well-being of your furry companions.

Ensuring proper pet care is not just a responsibility; it is a profound commitment to the well-being and happiness of our beloved animal companions. As pet owners, we are entrusted with the care and nurturing of these loyal creatures who bring immense joy and companionship.

The importance of pet care extends far beyond providing food and shelter. It is dedicated to meeting pets' physical, emotional, and social needs. Understanding and fulfilling these requirements can enhance our pets' quality of life and strengthen our bond with them.

Being a pet owner comes with many responsibilities, from routine grooming and exercise to regular veterinary visits and mental stimulation. However, the rewards of pet ownership are immeasurable. The unconditional love, companionship, and loyalty our pets offer us can profoundly enrich our lives.

By embracing the role of a pet owner with dedication and compassion, we ensure the health and well-being of our furry companions and create a nurturing and loving environment in which they can thrive. The pet care journey is filled with joy, challenges, and endless growth opportunities for us and our beloved pets.

Daily Care Routine: Detail the essential aspects of daily pet care, including feeding schedules, grooming routines, exercise requirements, and mental stimulation

Caring for your pet daily is not just a duty—it's an opportunity to strengthen your bond and ensure their happiness and well-being. A consistent routine is key to meeting your pet's physical and emotional needs. Here's a detailed guide to help you create a nurturing daily care routine for your furry companion:

Feeding schedules: Providing your pet with balanced and nutritious meals is essential for their health. Consult your veterinarian to determine the appropriate portion sizes and feeding times based on your pet's age, size, and breed. Offering fresh water at all times is also crucial to keep your pet hydrated.

Grooming routines: Regular grooming sessions are a chance to keep your pet looking their best and play a vital role in their health. Brushing your pet's coat helps prevent mats, distributes natural oils, and reduces shedding. Additionally, nail trimming, ear cleaning, and dental care should be incorporated into your pet's grooming routine to prevent potential health issues.

Exercise requirements: Physical activity is vital for your pet's well-being, as it helps maintain a healthy weight, promotes cardiovascular health, and prevents behavioral problems. Tailor your pet's exercise routine to their breed and energy level, ensuring they get enough daily exercise through walks, playtime, or interactive toys.

Mental stimulation: Keeping your pet mentally stimulated is as important as physical exercise. Enrich their environment with puzzle toys, interactive games, and training sessions to engage their minds and prevent boredom. Mental stimulation can help alleviate anxiety, boost cognitive function, and strengthen your bond with your pet.

Creating a nurturing environment: Your home should be your pet's safe and comfortable haven. Provide designated spaces for rest, play, and elimination, ensuring they have access to clean bedding, toys, and scratching posts. Establish a routine for bathroom breaks and ensure your pet has a secure environment to thrive in.

Incorporating these essential aspects of daily pet care into your routine ensures that your furry companion leads a happy, healthy, and fulfilling life. Remember, caring for a pet is a rewarding experience that enhances your life and theirs.

Veterinary Care and Health Maintenance: Emphasize the significance of regular veterinary check-ups, vaccinations, and preventive care

To ensure your beloved pet's optimal health and well-being, it is essential to prioritize regular veterinary check-ups, vaccinations, and preventive care. These proactive measures are crucial in detecting potential health issues early, allowing timely intervention and treatment.

Regular veterinary check-ups are a formality and a vital means of monitoring your pet's overall health. During these check-ups, your veterinarian can conduct thorough physical examinations, assess your pet's weight and dental health, and address any concerns you may have regarding your pet's well-being.

Vaccinations are another cornerstone of preventive pet care. Following a recommended vaccination schedule protects your pet from various contagious and potentially life-threatening diseases. Your veterinarian can guide you on the appropriate vaccinations for your pet based on age, lifestyle, and risk factors.

In addition to check-ups and vaccinations, it is paramount to be aware of common health issues in pets and recognize signs of illness. Symptoms such as changes in appetite, energy levels, behavior, or appearance should not be overlooked. Prompt veterinary attention can significantly affect your pet's prognosis and treatment outcomes.

Nutrition and exercise also play crucial roles in maintaining your pet's overall health and well-being. A balanced diet tailored to your pet's specific needs and regular exercise can help prevent obesity, promote healthy growth, and support an active lifestyle for your furry companion.

Proactive veterinary care, adherence to vaccination schedules, awareness of common health issues, and a focus on proper nutrition and exercise are fundamental to ensuring your pet's optimal health and well-being. By prioritizing these elements, you provide for your pet's physical health and foster a happy and fulfilling life for your cherished companion.

Establishing Meaningful Traditions

The holiday season is a time for coming together with loved ones, creating cherished memories, and building strong bonds that last a lifetime. Establishing meaningful traditions plays a crucial role in shaping these experiences and ensuring they hold a special place in our hearts for years. Whether it's a family recipe passed down through generations, a festive gathering that brings everyone closer, or a beloved ritual that defines the holiday spirit, traditions can enrich our lives and create a sense of continuity and connection.

These traditions serve as anchors in a fast-paced world, offering comfort, stability, and a sense of belonging. They remind us of who we are and where we come from, grounding us in our shared history and values. By honoring these traditions, we pay tribute to our heritage and create new memories that future generations will cherish.

Establishing meaningful traditions is not just about following a routine or going through the motions – it's about infusing each moment with intention and purpose. Whether it's a simple gesture like lighting candles together on Christmas Eve or a grand celebration that brings the whole family together, every tradition has the potential to deepen our connections and create lasting joy.

As we embrace the holiday season and look ahead to the future, let us remember the importance of these meaningful traditions in shaping our experiences and enriching our lives. Let us treasure the moments we share with loved ones, the traditions we hold dear, and the legacy we pass on to the next generation. In the tapestry of our lives, traditions are the threads that bind us together, creating a beautiful and enduring fabric of love and memories.

- Highlight the importance of creating lasting memories with loved ones through holiday traditions and family gatherings.

  The holiday season is a special time of year when families come together to create memories that will last a lifetime. One of the most meaningful ways to celebrate this time is by establishing traditions that bring loved ones closer

and strengthen the bonds of family unity. Whether it's decorating the Christmas tree together, preparing a special meal for Thanksgiving, or lighting the menorah during Hanukkah, these rituals help create a sense of belonging and continuity in our lives.

Holiday traditions provide a framework for shared experiences that can be passed down from generation to generation, creating a sense of connection with our past and hope for the future. These rituals offer a chance to slow down, reflect on what truly matters, and express gratitude for the love and support we receive from our family and friends.

Family gatherings during the holidays offer a unique opportunity to create memories that will be cherished for years to come whether it's playing games together, exchanging gifts, or simply sharing stories and laughter around the dinner table, these moments of togetherness help to strengthen our relationships and foster a sense of belonging.

In our fast-paced world, getting caught up in the hustle and bustle of the holiday season is easy. However, taking the time to establish meaningful traditions and prioritize family gatherings can help us refocus on what truly matters. These moments of connection and joy make the holiday season special and unforgettable for all involved.

- Discuss the significance of celebrating religious holidays and their role in family life.

  Celebrating religious holidays is deeply significant in family life, serving as a cornerstone for traditions and values passed down through generations. These special occasions provide a meaningful opportunity for families to come together in reflection and celebration, honoring their faith and heritage.

The observance of religious holidays offers a sense of continuity and connection to one's cultural and spiritual identity. It creates a sense of belonging and shared history among family members, fostering a bond transcending time and distance. Families can instill important values such as gratitude, empathy, and compassion in future generations through these sacred rituals and practices.

Moreover, religious holidays provide a framework for teaching children about their beliefs and customs, helping them understand and appreciate the significance of these traditions. Families can strengthen their sense of community and belonging by participating in religious ceremonies and rituals, reinforcing the importance of shared experiences and collective identity.

In the hustle and bustle of modern life, celebrating religious holidays offers a much-needed pause for reflection, gratitude, and spiritual renewal. It reminds us of the values and principles that guide our lives, grounding us in a sense of purpose and connection to something greater than ourselves.

As families navigate the complexities of budgeting for holiday events, it is essential to remember the profound significance of celebrating religious holidays in family life. Families can create lasting memories that enrich their relationships and deepen their bond by prioritizing these traditions and values.

Budgeting for Holiday and Family Events:

Celebrating holidays and family events is special, providing opportunities to create cherished memories and strengthen bonds with loved ones. However, the joy of these occasions can sometimes be overshadowed by financial worries. In this section, we will explore practical strategies for budgeting wisely to ensure that holiday celebrations remain enjoyable and fulfilling without causing undue financial strain.

1. Set Clear Priorities: When budgeting for holiday and family events, it is essential to identify your priorities and allocate funds accordingly. Consider what aspects of the celebration are most meaningful to you and your family, whether it's gathering for a festive meal, exchanging heartfelt gifts, or traveling to be together. By focusing on what truly matters, you can make informed decisions about where to allocate your budget.

2. Create a Holiday Budget: Establishing a dedicated holiday budget can help you manage expenses and avoid overspending. Start by listing all anticipated costs, including gifts,

decorations, food, travel, and other related expenses. Assign specific amounts to each category based on your budget and financial goals. Be realistic in your estimates and ensure that your budget aligns with your financial capabilities.

3. Plan: Planning is key to successful holiday budgeting. Start saving for holiday expenses early in the year, setting aside a portion of your monthly income to build a holiday fund. By spreading out the costs over time, you can simultaneously alleviate the financial burden of large expenses. Additionally, plan your holiday shopping and activities to take advantage of sales and discounts, maximizing your savings.

4. Embrace Creativity: Budgeting for holiday and family events does not mean sacrificing joy or celebration. Get creative with gift-giving by making personalized presents or opting for thoughtful gestures with sentimental value. Look for budget-friendly decorating ideas and activities the whole family can enjoy

without breaking the bank. Remember that the true spirit of the holidays lies in the time spent together, not the price tag of gifts or decorations.

5. Seek Alternative Ways to Celebrate: Consider alternative ways to celebrate holidays and family events that align with your budget constraints. Host a potluck gathering where everyone contributes a dish, organize a family DIY crafting session to create decorations, or plan a nature outing for a memorable experience that doesn't rely on expensive purchases. Focus on the intangible aspects of celebration, such as togetherness and gratitude, to create lasting memories without financial stress.

By approaching holiday and family events and budgeting thoughtfully and strategically, you can enjoy meaningful celebrations while staying within your financial means. Remember that the value of these occasions lies not in the price of gifts or extravagance but in the joy of shared experiences and cherished traditions.

- Provide practical budgeting tips effectively for holiday expenses, including gifts, decorations, and travel costs.

  As we approach the holiday season, planning and budgeting effectively is essential to ensure a joyful celebration without financial stress. Here are some practical tips to help you manage holiday expenses wisely:

1. Set a Realistic Budget: Start by determining how much you can spend on gifts, decorations, and travel costs without compromising your overall financial goals. Consider your current financial situation and establish a clear budget to guide your holiday spending.

2. Make a List and Prioritize: List all the holiday expenses you anticipate, including gifts for family and friends, decorations for your home, travel expenses, and any additional costs. Prioritize these expenses based on their importance to you and allocate funds accordingly.

3. Research and Compare Prices: Before making any purchases, take the time to research prices and compare options. Look for sales, discounts, and special offers to maximize your budget and get the most value for your money. Consider shopping online for convenience and potentially lower prices.

4. Plan Ahead for Travel: Book your transportation and accommodations in advance to secure the best rates if you travel during the holidays. Consider flexible travel dates to take advantage of lower prices and avoid peak travel times.

5. DIY and Personalize Gifts: Get creative and consider making homemade gifts or personalizing presents for your loved ones. Not only can DIY gifts be more meaningful, but they can also be more cost-effective than store-bought items.

6. Limit Impulse Purchases: Stay disciplined and avoid impulse buying during the holiday season. Stick to your budget and resist the temptation to overspend on unnecessary items. Remember that

thoughtful gestures and experiences often hold more value than material possessions.

7. Monitor Your Spending: Track your holiday expenses throughout the season to ensure you stay within your budget. Review your purchases regularly and make adjustments as needed to stay manageable.

By following these practical tips and staying mindful of your financial boundaries, you can create a memorable holiday season filled with joy and celebration, all while maintaining financial peace of mind.

- Emphasize setting financial boundaries while enjoying special occasions with family and friends.
  Setting financial boundaries while enjoying special occasions with family and friends is crucial to maintaining financial health and meaningful relationships. Prioritizing your budgetary constraints and your desire to celebrate special occasions with loved ones is essential.

One effective way to emphasize the importance of setting financial boundaries is to plan ahead and create a detailed budget specifically for holiday expenses. Start by identifying your overall spending limit for gifts, decorations, and travel costs, and allocate amounts for each category based on your financial capacity.

Communicating openly with family and friends about your budget constraints can help manage expectations and prevent unnecessary overspending. Be honest about your financial boundaries and express your desire to enjoy the holiday season without jeopardizing your long-term financial goals.

When pressured to overspend or exceed your budget, remember that true joy and connection during special occasions come from being present with loved ones, not from extravagant gifts or lavish celebrations. Focus on creating meaningful experiences and fostering relationships rather than solely on materialistic aspects of the holiday season.

By setting clear financial boundaries and communicating effectively with your loved ones, you can strike a balance between enjoying special occasions and maintaining financial stability. Remember that the true essence of holidays lies in the joy of shared experiences and precious moments spent with those who matter most.

Balancing Family Expectations and Financial Realities:

Navigating the delicate balance between meeting family expectations and staying true to your financial goals can be challenging yet crucial to managing your budget during the holiday season. While the desire to create magical moments for your loved ones is understandable, it's essential to prioritize financial stability and responsibility.

One effective strategy for achieving this balance is to open up a dialogue with your family about your financial limitations without dampening the festive spirit. Communicating openly and honestly about your budget constraints can help set realistic expectations and foster understanding among family members.

Another helpful approach is to set clear financial boundaries and establish a holiday spending plan that aligns with your overall financial goals.

By outlining your budget for gifts, travel, and other holiday expenses in advance, you can ensure that your financial resources are allocated wisely and prevent overspending.

It's also essential to focus on the meaningful experiences and traditions that bring joy during the holiday season rather than solely on material gifts or extravagant activities. Emphasizing the value of quality time spent together and creating lasting memories can shift the focus from expensive purchases to heartfelt connections.

Balancing family expectations and maintaining financial stability requires careful planning, clear communication, and a willingness to prioritize your long-term financial well-being. By approaching holiday spending with a strategic mindset and a commitment to financial responsibility, you can enjoy special moments with your loved ones while staying true to your financial goals.

- Explore ways to navigate the pressure of meeting family expectations for holiday spending while staying true to your financial goals.

During the holiday season, there is often a heightened sense of obligation to meet family expectations when it comes to spending. The pressure to create the perfect holiday experience can lead to financial strain and stress for many individuals and families. However, it is important to remember that staying true to your financial goals and priorities is paramount, even during this festive time.

Setting clear and realistic expectations is one key strategy in balancing family expectations with financial realities. Communicating openly and honestly with your family about your budget constraints can help manage their expectations and reduce potential conflicts or misunderstandings. Having these conversations early on establishes boundaries and sets the tone for a financially responsible holiday season.

Another approach is to focus on the true meaning of the holidays and shift the emphasis away from extravagant gifts and lavish celebrations. Encourage meaningful experiences and quality time together rather than measuring the season's success based on material possessions. This can help alleviate the pressure to overspend and instead foster a sense of joy and gratitude that does not depend on the size of your budget.

Additionally, be proactive in finding creative and budget-friendly ways to celebrate the holidays. Consider hosting a potluck gathering where everyone contributes a dish or organizing a gift exchange to reduce the financial burden of buying individual gifts for every family member. Embrace DIY decorations and homemade gifts as thoughtful and personal alternatives to store-bought items.

Above all, remember that the holidays are about coming together with loved ones, creating cherished memories, and celebrating the season's spirit. By approaching the challenge of meeting family expectations for holiday spending with a focus on financial responsibility and open communication, you can navigate this potentially stressful time with grace and joy.

- Offer strategies for communicating openly and honestly with family members about budget constraints without sacrificing the season's joy.

Navigating the delicate balance between meeting family expectations for holiday spending and staying true to your financial goals can be challenging. Communicating openly and honestly with your family members about your budget constraints is essential while preserving the season's joy.

One effective strategy is initiating a conversation with your loved ones before the holiday. By discussing your financial limitations early on, you can set clear expectations and avoid misunderstandings later. Be transparent about your budgetary constraints and provide insight into the reasons behind your decisions.

Another helpful approach is to involve your family members in the budgeting process. Encourage open dialogue about how to allocate funds for gifts, decorations, and other holiday expenses. You can foster collaboration and shared responsibility by including your loved ones in the decision-making process.

Additionally, consider setting boundaries and establishing priorities for holiday spending. Communicate the importance of focusing on meaningful experiences rather than material possessions. Suggest creative alternatives, such as homemade gifts or budget-friendly activities, to make the holiday season special without breaking the bank.

Above all, emphasize the value of quality time spent together as a family. Remind your loved ones that the true joy of the season lies in creating cherished memories and strengthening relationships rather than in extravagant gifts or lavish displays. Communicating openly and honestly with your family members about your budget constraints allows you to navigate the holiday season with financial wisdom and genuine joy.

Socializing Expenses

Regarding socializing expenses, one significant area to consider is dining out. Dining out entails delicious meals at restaurants, cafes, and bars. While dining out offers convenience and a break from cooking at home, it also comes with a price tag.

The costs associated with dining out can vary based on the type of establishment, the cuisine served, and the frequency of dining out. Fine dining restaurants may offer exquisite dishes and a luxurious ambiance, but they often come with a higher price point. On the other hand, casual cafes and fast-food joints provide more budget-friendly options for those looking to grab a quick bite.

When budgeting for dining out expenses, it's essential to consider the cost of the meal and additional expenses such as taxes, tips, and beverages. Opting for water instead of pricey drinks can help keep costs down. Additionally, being mindful of portion sizes and avoiding unnecessary add-ons can save costs.

Setting a realistic budget for dining-out expenses and tracking spending regularly can help manage them effectively. Planning and choosing affordable dining options can help ensure that socializing over meals remains enjoyable without breaking the bank.

While dining out can be a delightful way to socialize and enjoy good food, being conscious of the costs is key to maintaining a balanced budget. With thoughtful planning and mindful spending, one can savor the experience of dining out while keeping financial goals in check.

- Dining Out: Discuss the costs of eating out at restaurants, cafes, and bars. When dining out, it's essential to consider the costs associated with indulging in meals at restaurants, cafes, and bars. While dining out can be a delightful experience, it's wise to be mindful of expenses to ensure your budget remains balanced.

The cost of dining out can vary significantly depending on the type of establishment you choose. Fine-dining restaurants typically have a higher price tag than casual cafes or fast-food joints. Factors such as the menu offerings, ambiance, and location can all impact the overall cost of your meal.

In addition to the actual food and beverages, it's important to factor in other expenses that may arise while dining out. These can include tips for service staff, taxes, and additional charges like corkage fees for bringing your wine to the restaurant.

To effectively manage dining out expenses, consider setting a budget and sticking to it for how often you dine out each month. You may also explore ways to save money while enjoying the experience, such as opting for lunch specials, happy hour deals, or dining at off-peak hours when prices are lower.

Ultimately, dining out can be a pleasurable and convenient way to enjoy delicious meals and socialize. By being mindful of costs and making informed choices, you can savor dining-out experiences without breaking the bank.

- Entertainment Activities: Explore expenses related to movies, concerts, sporting events, and other social outings.

In today's fast-paced lifestyle, entertainment activities play a significant role in providing relaxation and rejuvenation. Whether it's catching the latest blockbuster movie, attending a live concert, or cheering for your favorite team at a sporting event, these social outings bring joy and excitement to our lives. However, indulging in such activities has a financial cost to consider in your budget planning.

Movies are a timeless form of entertainment, offering various options, from blockbuster releases to independent films. The cost of movie tickets, concessions, and any additional fees can add up, especially if you frequent the theaters regularly. To manage expenses effectively, consider alternatives such as matinee showings, discount days, or subscription services like streaming platforms.

Concerts and live performances are another popular entertainment choice for many individuals. Ticket prices vary based on the artist or venue, from concerts to theater shows. Budgeting for ticket costs and factors like parking fees, merchandise purchases, and refreshments at the event is essential.

Attending games and matches can be a thrilling experience for sports enthusiasts. Whether it's a local team or a major league event, expenses include ticket prices, transportation to the venue, game-day snacks, and souvenirs. To stay within your budget, consider looking for promotions, ticket discounts, or less expensive seating options.

While entertainment activities provide enjoyment and social interaction, it is crucial to plan for these expenses wisely. By including these costs in your budget and exploring money-saving strategies, you can continue to engage in these enriching experiences without compromising your financial goals. Balancing entertainment activities with other budget priorities will help you maintain a healthy financial lifestyle while enjoying the pleasures that entertainment has to offer.

- Social Events: Cover costs of attending parties, gatherings, and special occasions.

Attending social events is a delightful way to connect with friends, family, and acquaintances, but it's essential to be mindful of the costs associated with these gatherings. Whether it's a birthday party, a wedding reception, or a holiday celebration, attending parties and special occasions can add up quickly in terms of expenses.

The costs of attending social events can vary depending on the type of occasion and your level of involvement. Consider expenses such as gifts or contributions for the host, attire or outfits for the event, transportation to and from the venue, and any additional expenses such as drinks or food if not provided. Budgeting accordingly is important to avoid financial strain while enjoying these social gatherings.

One way to manage costs related to social events is to plan and prioritize the events that are most important to you. Choose events that align with your interests and values, and consider setting a budget for each occasion to keep track of your spending. Additionally, carpooling or sharing transportation costs with friends can help reduce expenses while allowing you to participate in social events.

Remember that attending parties, gatherings, and special occasions can be a fun and rewarding experience, but it's also essential to be mindful of the financial aspect. By proactively planning and budgeting for social events, you can enjoy these special moments without overspending and stay within your financial goals.

Travel and Vacation Expenses:

When planning your travel and vacation expenses, it is crucial to consider all aspects of your journey to ensure a seamless and enjoyable experience. From transportation costs to accommodation expenses and sightseeing activities, every detail significantly shapes your travel budget.

Transportation costs encompass a wide range of expenses, including flights, trains, rental cars, and other means of travel. Researching and comparing prices is essential to find the most cost-effective and convenient transportation options for your trip. Booking in advance or looking for deals and promotions can help you save money on transportation expenses.

Accommodation expenses are another essential factor to consider when budgeting for your travel. Whether you choose to stay in hotels, Airbnb rentals, or other lodging options, setting a budget and exploring different accommodation choices that meet your needs and preferences is essential. Consider location, amenities, and reviews when selecting accommodation to ensure a comfortable and enjoyable stay.

Sightseeing and activities are vital in shaping your travel experience and budget. From guided tours and attractions to recreational activities and cultural experiences, there are plenty of opportunities to explore and enjoy during your trip. Researching and planning your itinerary can help you prioritize activities and allocate funds accordingly to make the most of your travel experience.

By carefully considering transportation costs, accommodation expenses, and sightseeing activities, you can create a comprehensive budget for your travel and vacation expenses.

Remember to factor in additional costs such as meals, souvenirs, and unforeseen expenses to ensure a well-rounded and stress-free travel experience. Planning and staying organized can help you make the most of your travel budget and create lasting memories during your journey.

- Transportation Costs: Detail expenses for flights, trains, rental cars, and other travel means.
  Transportation Costs play a significant role in the overall budgeting process for travel and vacations. When planning a trip, it is essential to factor in the expenses associated with flights, trains, rental cars, and other travel means to ensure a realistic and accurate budget.

Flights are often one of the most substantial transportation expenses, especially long-distance travel. The cost of airfare can vary depending on the destination, time of booking, and airline choice. To save on flight expenses, it is advisable to book tickets in advance, consider flying on less popular days or times, and compare prices from different airlines.

Trains offer a convenient and scenic way to travel, particularly in regions with efficient rail networks. The cost of train tickets can vary based on the travel distance, class of service, and type of train. Booking train tickets early or taking advantage of special promotions can help lower transportation costs while enjoying a comfortable journey.

Rental cars provide flexibility and freedom to explore different destinations during a trip. The cost of renting a car can vary depending on the rental company, type of vehicle, duration of rental, and insurance coverage. It is essential to compare rental car prices, consider additional fees or surcharges, and book in advance to secure the best deal.

Other travel means, such as buses, ferries, or local transportation services, also contribute to transportation costs during a vacation. These expenses can add up, especially if traveling to multiple locations or relying on public transportation extensively. Planning, researching transportation options, and budgeting for these costs can help manage expenses effectively.

By carefully considering transportation costs in your travel budget, you can allocate resources efficiently, maximize your travel experiences, and ensure a well-rounded and enjoyable trip without overspending.

- Accommodation Expenses: Discuss the costs of hotels, Airbnb rentals, and other lodging options.
  Accommodation during travel is a crucial aspect to consider when planning your expenses. Whether you prefer the convenience of hotels, the personalized experience of Airbnb rentals, or other lodging options, it's essential to budget for this significant expense.

Hotels offer a range of accommodations, from budget-friendly options to luxury suites. The cost of a hotel room can vary based on factors such as location, amenities, and seasonality. Consider factors like proximity to attractions, safety, and reviews when selecting a hotel within your budget.

Airbnb rentals provide a unique experience by allowing travelers to stay in private homes, apartments, or unique properties. Factors like location, size, and amenities offered can influence the cost of an Airbnb rental. It's essential to read reviews, verify the host's credibility, and communicate specific requirements before booking an Airbnb property.

Other lodging options, such as hostels, bed and breakfasts, or vacation rentals, offer alternatives to traditional hotels and Airbnb rentals. Depending on your preferences, these accommodations may provide cost savings or a more personalized experience.

Consider the nightly rate and additional costs like taxes, service fees, and security deposits when budgeting for accommodation expenses. Remember that prices may fluctuate based on demand, availability, and seasonal factors.

By carefully planning and budgeting for accommodation expenses, you can ensure a comfortable and enjoyable stay while staying within your financial means. Remember to prioritize safety, comfort, and convenience when selecting accommodations to maximize your travel experience.

- Sightseeing and Activities: Explore travel expenses related to tours, attractions, and recreational activities.

  When traveling, exploring the sights and engaging in various activities can add a delightful dimension to your experience. However, these activities often come with associated expenses that must be considered in your budget planning.

Sightseeing and activities while traveling encompass a wide range of experiences, from visiting iconic landmarks to participating in adventurous excursions. Each activity offers a unique glimpse into the culture and attractions of the destination, providing memories that last a lifetime.

When budgeting for sightseeing and activities, it is essential to research the costs associated with popular tours, attractions, and recreational opportunities at your destination. Ticket prices, guided tour fees, admission charges, and equipment rentals should all be factored into your budget to ensure a comprehensive overview of expenses.

Additionally, consider any transportation expenses required to reach these attractions, such as public transportation fares or rental car fees. Planning your itinerary efficiently can help minimize transport costs and maximize your time spent enjoying the sights and activities.

To maximize your travel budget, seek discounted tickets or bundled tour packages that offer savings on multiple attractions. Many destinations offer tourist passes that provide access to a selection of popular attractions at a reduced rate, making it a cost-effective option for sightseeing.

Remember to allocate a portion of your budget for unexpected activities or spontaneous opportunities that may arise during your travels. Flexibility in your budget will allow you to accommodate impromptu excursions or unique experiences that enrich your journey.

By carefully considering the expenses related to sightseeing and activities while traveling and incorporating them into your budget plan, you can enjoy a fulfilling travel experience without compromising your financial well-being.

Hobbies and Recreation Costs:

Engaging in hobbies and recreational activities is not just a way to pass the time; it is an essential aspect of self-care and personal fulfillment. Whether you enjoy painting, gardening, or playing a musical instrument, pursuing your hobbies can bring joy and relaxation. However, indulging in these activities often comes with a cost. This section will delve into the financial aspects of hobbies and recreation, discussing the expenses associated with equipment, materials, and tools.

When it comes to hobbies, the costs can vary significantly depending on the nature of the activity. For some, the expenses may be minimal, requiring only basic supplies like paints and brushes for painting or seeds and soil for gardening. Others may involve more specialized equipment or tools, such as a guitar for playing music or a sewing machine for crafting.

Investing in quality supplies is crucial for enjoying your hobbies to the fullest. While it can be tempting to opt for cheaper alternatives, skimping on quality can often lead to frustration and a diminished experience. Consider the long-term benefits of purchasing durable and reliable materials that will enhance your skills and enjoyment in the long run.

Additionally, remember that maintaining and upgrading your hobby equipment may be necessary over time. Regular maintenance, such as sharpening tools or replacing worn-out parts, can extend the lifespan of your supplies and ensure smooth functionality. Budgeting for these maintenance costs is essential to preserve the longevity of your hobby materials.

Furthermore, exploring new hobbies or recreational activities may require investing in classes or workshops to develop your skills further. While these educational opportunities come with a price tag, the knowledge and expertise gained can enrich your experience and broaden your horizons in your chosen hobby.

While hobbies and recreation costs may seem like discretionary expenses, they play a vital role in enhancing one's well-being and overall satisfaction in life. By budgeting responsibly and prioritizing quality materials and educational opportunities, one can fully enjoy the benefits of one's hobbies while maintaining financial stability.

- Hobby Supplies: Discuss expenses for equipment, materials, and tools related to hobbies and recreational activities. Engaging in hobbies and recreational activities is a wonderful way to unwind, explore new interests, and hone our skills. However, pursuing these passions often comes with its associated costs. This section will delve into hobby supplies and discuss the expenses of acquiring equipment, materials, and tools necessary for engaging in various hobbies.

When it comes to hobbies, the range of supplies required can vary greatly depending on the activity. For those who enjoy crafting, painting, or DIY projects, the costs may include paintbrushes, canvases, woodworking tools, and specialty materials. These supplies are essential for bringing creative ideas to life and achieving desired results in artistic endeavors.

Similarly, individuals interested in sports and outdoor activities may invest in hiking boots, fishing rods, camping equipment, or sports attire. These items enhance the overall experience and ensure safety and comfort while engaging in physical pursuits.

Furthermore, technology enthusiasts often find themselves drawn to gadgets, software, and tools that facilitate their hobbies, whether photography, coding, or music production. The expenses of acquiring the latest cameras, editing software, or musical instruments can add up but are considered valuable investments in pursuing one's passion.

Budgeting and planning for hobby supplies is important to ensure a fulfilling and sustainable engagement with our recreational activities. Researching and comparing prices, taking advantage of discounts and sales, and prioritizing essentials over luxuries can help manage costs effectively. Additionally, exploring second-hand options, borrowing from friends, or participating in community-sharing programs can provide affordable alternatives to acquiring necessary supplies.

While pursuing hobbies is rewarding, it is essential to be mindful of the expenses of obtaining hobby supplies. By carefully managing and budgeting for these costs, individuals can continue to nurture their passions and interests without compromising their financial well-being.

- Membership and Subscriptions: Detail costs associated with club memberships, subscription services, and online platforms.

    Membership and subscriptions play a vital role in enhancing one's hobbies and recreational pursuits. These costs encompass club memberships, subscription services, and online platforms that offer unique opportunities and resources for individuals to indulge in their interests.

Individuals commit to joining exclusive groups or organizations that align with their hobbies or recreational preferences when considering club memberships. These memberships often provide access to specialized facilities, events, and networking opportunities that can enrich one's experience and skills within one's chosen hobby. While the initial cost of joining a club may seem steep, the benefits and sense of community derived from such memberships are invaluable.

On the other hand, subscription services offer a convenient way to access a wide range of resources tailored to specific hobbies and interests. Whether it be a monthly magazine subscription, a digital platform for tutorials and guides, or a curated box of supplies delivered to your door, these services provide a steady stream of inspiration and tools to fuel your passion. While the cumulative cost of multiple subscriptions may add up, their convenience and curated content can significantly enhance one's hobby experience.

Online platforms have revolutionized how individuals engage with their hobbies and recreational interests. From virtual classes and workshops to online communities and forums, these platforms provide many resources and opportunities for skill development and interaction with like-minded enthusiasts. While some online platforms offer free resources, premium memberships may unlock additional features and benefits that cater to more serious hobbyists.

Investing in club memberships, subscription services, and online platforms can elevate your hobby pursuits. While these costs may require careful budgeting and consideration, the enrichment and fulfillment they provide in pursuing your passions are well worth the investment.

- Recreational Classes: Cover expenses for classes, workshops, and lessons to pursue hobbies and recreational interests.

    Engaging in recreational classes is not just a way to learn new skills; it's an investment in your personal growth and well-being. Whether you're passionate about painting, dancing, cooking, or photography, enrolling in classes and workshops tailored to your interests can provide a fulfilling and enriching experience.

When considering the expenses associated with recreational classes, it is essential to focus on the value they bring to your life. While the cost of these classes may vary depending on the duration, level of expertise, and materials required, the benefits often outweigh the financial investment.

Pursuing hobbies and recreational interests through structured classes allows you to learn from experienced instructors, interact with like-minded individuals, and hone your skills in a supportive environment. The sense of accomplishment and satisfaction from mastering a new technique or creating something beautiful is priceless.

Moreover, recreational classes provide invaluable mental and emotional benefits. They offer a creative outlet and a break from daily stressors and contribute to personal growth, self-confidence, and overall well-being. By dedicating time and resources to nurturing your passions, you commit to your happiness and fulfillment.

When budgeting for recreational classes, consider the long-term impact they can have on your life. While allocating funds for these experiences is essential, remember that the knowledge and skills you gain can lead to new opportunities, friendships, and meaningful experiences. Investing in yourself through recreational classes is not just a transaction; it's an investment in a more inspired and enriched life.

Analyzing Debt Obligations

When analyzing debt obligations, it is imperative to have a comprehensive understanding of the types of debt one may hold. Debt can manifest in various forms, such as credit card debt, student loans, mortgages, car loans, and personal loans. Each type of debt comes with its terms, interest rates, and repayment structures, which necessitate careful evaluation.

Moreover, the importance of debt management must be balanced. Unchecked debt can lead to a downward spiral of financial insecurity, stress, and limitations on one's ability to achieve long-term financial goals. By analyzing and assessing debt obligations, individuals can gain clarity on their financial standing and take proactive steps toward achieving financial stability.

One key metric in this analysis is the debt-to-income ratio. This ratio provides insight into how much of an individual's income is used to service debt obligations. A high debt-to-income ratio may indicate an individual is overleveraged and could be at risk of financial distress. By calculating this ratio, individuals can pinpoint areas they may need to adjust to improve their financial health.

Analyzing debt obligations is the first step towards regaining control of one's financial well-being. By delving into the specifics of one's debts, understanding the implications of each type of debt, and evaluating the debt-to-income ratio, individuals can lay the groundwork for effective debt management strategies and pave the way toward a more secure financial future.

Strategies for Managing Debt

Creating a structured plan that aligns with your financial goals is crucial to managing debt effectively. Here are some strategies to help you navigate and overcome your debt obligations:

1. Create a Debt Payoff Plan: List all your debts, including the amount owed and the interest rates. Develop a realistic timeline for paying off each debt, considering your income and expenses. Prioritize debts with the highest interest rates to minimize the amount of interest paid over time.

2. Prioritize High-Interest Debts: Focus on paying off high-interest debts first, as they can quickly accumulate and become a significant financial burden. By tackling these debts early on, you can save money on interest payments and expedite your journey towards becoming debt-free.

3. Negotiate with Creditors: If you struggle to pay certain debts, consider contacting creditors to discuss potential repayment options. Many creditors are willing to negotiate payment plans or settle for a reduced amount to help you eliminate your debt. Being proactive and transparent about your financial situation can lead to more manageable debt repayment terms.

By implementing these strategies and staying committed to your debt payoff plan, you can take control of your financial situation and work towards a debt-free future. Remember that managing debt requires discipline and persistence, but the rewards of financial freedom are well worth the effort.

Long-Term Financial Impact of Debt

Debt significantly impacts one's long-term financial well-being, shaping financial stability and opportunities for growth. Understanding the long-term consequences of debt is crucial in making informed financial decisions and planning for a secure future.

One of debt's most apparent long-term impacts is its effect on credit scores. Consistent and timely debt repayment can positively influence your credit score, opening doors to favorable interest rates on loans, credit cards, and potential employment opportunities. On the contrary, defaulting on debt payments or carrying high levels of debt relative to income can damage your credit score, hindering your ability to secure financing or obtain competitive interest rates.

Moreover, the debt burden can extend beyond the immediate financial strain and impede your progress toward long-term financial goals. High debt levels can limit your ability to save for retirement, invest in assets that appreciate over time, or pursue significant life milestones such as buying a home or starting a business. By reducing debt and managing it effectively, individuals can free up resources to allocate towards savings and investments and build a solid financial foundation for the future.

Additionally, carrying excessive debt can subject individuals to financial stress and uncertainty, impacting overall well-being and quality of life. The weight of debt can strain relationships, lead to sleepless nights, and contribute to feelings of anxiety and insecurity about the future. Taking proactive steps to address and manage debt can alleviate this stress, providing peace of mind and enhancing overall financial health.

In conclusion, recognizing the long-term financial implications of debt is essential for establishing a sustainable financial future. By prioritizing debt management, improving credit scores, and reducing financial stress, individuals can position themselves for greater financial security, increased opportunities, and a brighter financial outlook in the years to come.

Importance of Insurance in Financial Planning

Insurance plays a pivotal role in financial planning, critical in safeguarding one's assets and mitigating potential risks. Whether it be protecting a home against unforeseen disasters, insuring a vehicle to cover accidents, or securing health coverage for medical expenses, insurance is vital in ensuring stability and peace of mind in one's financial journey.

Understanding the significance of insurance in financial planning involves recognizing the value it brings in shielding individuals and families from financial turbulence. By transferring risks to an insurance provider, individuals can safeguard themselves against unexpected events leading to significant financial losses. This proactive approach helps manage uncertainties and provides a sense of security and protection for the future.

Moreover, insurance ensures financial well-being by providing a safety net to help individuals recover from challenging situations. Whether replacing lost income due to disability, covering medical expenses in times of illness, or compensating for property damage, insurance offers protection that can prevent financial setbacks from spiraling out of control.

Insurance plays a dual role in risk management and wealth preservation in the broader scope of financial planning. By strategically selecting insurance policies that align with one's unique circumstances and financial goals, individuals can fortify their financial foundation and create a safety net that shields them from potential risks in the long run. Considering insurance as a fundamental aspect of financial planning can help individuals confidently navigate uncertainties and build a resilient financial future.

Factors to Consider When Choosing Insurance Policies

Several key factors should be carefully considered when choosing insurance policies to ensure that individuals are adequately protected while effectively managing costs.

One important factor to consider is the type of coverage needed based on individual circumstances. Assessing one's specific risks and potential liabilities can help determine the appropriate types of insurance policies to prioritize. For example, individuals with dependents may need life insurance to provide financial protection for their loved ones in the event of their passing.

Another crucial factor is the coverage limits and deductibles offered by different insurance policies. Evaluating the level of coverage needed to mitigate potential risks and calculating the affordability of premiums and deductibles can help individuals strike a balance between protection and cost.

The insurance provider's reputation and financial stability should also be considered when choosing insurance policies. Selecting a reputable and financially sound insurance company can provide peace of mind, knowing that claims will be paid out promptly and efficiently when needed.

Moreover, reviewing the exclusions and limitations of insurance policies is essential to ensure that individuals understand what is covered and what is not. Reading the fine print and seeking clarification on ambiguous terms can help prevent misunderstandings and ensure that expectations align with the coverage provided.

Lastly, seeking advice from a trusted insurance agent or financial advisor can be beneficial when choosing insurance policies. Professionals can offer personalized recommendations based on individual needs and help navigate the complexities of insurance options to make informed decisions.

When choosing insurance policies, considering these factors can help individuals tailor their coverage to align with their specific needs and budget while providing the necessary protection for themselves and their loved ones.

Strategies for Optimizing Insurance Costs

When it comes to optimizing insurance costs, there are several strategies that individuals can consider to ensure they are getting the best coverage at the most affordable price. By being proactive and strategic in your insurance approach, you can save money without sacrificing the level of protection you need. Here are some tips and strategies to help you optimize your insurance costs:

1. Shop Around: One of the most effective ways to save on insurance costs is to shop around and compare quotes from different insurance providers. You can get the best price for the coverage you need by obtaining multiple quotes. It's important to consider factors beyond the premium cost, such as coverage limits, deductibles, and customer service reputation.

2. Bundle Policies: Many insurance companies offer discounts for bundling multiple policies, such as auto and home insurance. By consolidating your insurance needs with one provider, you can save money on your overall premiums. Be sure to inquire about bundling options when obtaining quotes from insurance companies.

3. Review Coverage Needs: Regularly reviewing your insurance coverage needs can help avoid paying for unnecessary coverage. When evaluating your needed coverage, consider your current life stage, financial situation, and assets. Adjusting your coverage levels to reflect

your circumstances can help you save on premiums.

4. Increase Deductibles: Another way to lower your insurance premiums is to increase your deductibles. A higher deductible means you will pay more out of pocket in the event of a claim, but it can also lead to lower premium costs. Ensure you can afford the higher deductible if you need to file a claim.

5. Maintain a Good Credit Score: In some states, insurance companies use credit scores to determine premiums. Maintaining a good credit score may make you eligible for lower insurance rates. Paying bills on time, reducing debt, and monitoring your credit report can all help improve your credit score.

6. Take Advantage of Discounts: Many insurance companies offer various discounts that policyholders can use to save money. These discounts may be based on driving record, age, occupation, or membership in certain organizations.

Be sure to inquire about any discounts you qualify for when obtaining quotes.

By implementing these strategies and proactively managing your insurance costs, you can ensure you get the best value for your insurance premiums. Remember to review your coverage regularly, compare quotes from different providers, and use cost-saving opportunities to optimize your insurance costs while maintaining the coverage you need.

Introduction to Investing and Retirement Planning

Investing and retirement planning are crucial aspects of financial stability and security for individuals. By effectively allocating funds into various investment vehicles, one can build wealth over time and ensure a comfortable retirement.

There are various types of investing to consider. Stocks represent ownership in a company and have the potential for high returns but also come with higher risk. On the other hand, bonds are debt securities issued by corporations or governments, providing a fixed income stream but with lower returns than stocks. Mutual funds pool money from multiple investors to invest in a diversified portfolio of securities, offering a convenient way to access professional money management.

Assessing your risk tolerance and investment goals before choosing where to allocate your funds is essential. Diversification, or spreading investments across different asset classes and industries, can help mitigate risk and optimize returns. Understanding the fundamentals of each investment type and how they fit into your overall financial plan is key to building a robust investment portfolio.

Setting clear financial goals and timelines is essential in retirement planning. Whether you're saving for retirement through employer-sponsored plans like 401(k)s or individual retirement accounts (IRAs), having a structured approach to saving and investing for retirement is paramount. Regularly reviewing and adjusting your retirement plan based on changing circumstances and market conditions is crucial to staying on track toward your retirement goals.

Individuals can take proactive steps towards securing their financial future and enjoying a comfortable retirement by delving into investing and retirement planning. It is never too early to start planning and investing wisely to build a solid financial foundation for the years ahead.

Types of Investments

Explanation of Different Investment Vehicles:

Investing is essential to financial planning, allowing individuals to grow their wealth over time. Various investment vehicles are available to investors, each with its own unique characteristics and risk profiles. Understanding the different types of investments is crucial in building a diversified portfolio that aligns with your financial goals and risk tolerance.

1. Stocks: Stocks represent ownership in a company and are one of the most common investment vehicles. When you purchase a stock, you become a shareholder in the company and may benefit from its growth through capital appreciation and dividends. Stocks offer the potential for high returns but also come with higher volatility and risk.

2. Bonds: Bonds are debt securities issued by corporations or governments to raise capital. When you invest in a bond, you are lending money to the issuer in exchange for regular interest payments and the return of the principal amount at maturity. Bonds are considered less risky than stocks and provide a predictable

income stream, making them a popular choice for conservative investors.

3. Mutual Funds: Mutual funds pool money from multiple investors to invest in a diversified portfolio of stocks, bonds, or other securities. Professional fund managers make investment decisions on behalf of fund investors, offering diversification and professional management. Mutual funds come in various types, such as index, actively managed, and sector-specific funds, catering to different investment objectives.

4. Exchange-Traded Funds (ETFs): ETFs are similar to mutual funds but trade on stock exchanges like individual stocks. ETFs offer diversification, liquidity, and low expense ratios, making them a cost-effective investment option for investors seeking broad market exposure or specific asset classes.

5. Real Estate Investment Trusts (REITs): REITs own, operate, or finance income-producing real estate across various

sectors, such as residential, commercial, or industrial properties. Investing in REITs provides a way to gain exposure to the real estate market without directly owning physical properties. REITs typically offer attractive dividend yields and can serve as a diversification tool in a portfolio.

By understanding different investment vehicles' characteristics and risk profiles, investors can make informed decisions that align with their financial goals and risk tolerance. Diversification across various asset classes can help mitigate risk and enhance long-term returns, making a well-rounded investment strategy crucial for financial success.

- Explanation of different investment vehicles (stocks, bonds, mutual funds, etc.)

  In the world of investing, there are several types of investment vehicles that individuals can utilize to grow their wealth and secure their financial future. Understanding the characteristics and potential benefits of each type of investment is crucial for making informed decisions about where to allocate your money.

1. Stocks: Stocks represent ownership in a company and are bought and sold on stock exchanges. When you purchase a stock, you become a shareholder in the company, entitling you to a portion of its profits (dividends) and potential capital gains through the stock's price appreciation. Investing in stocks carries a higher risk than other asset classes, but historically, stocks have provided higher returns over the long term.

2. Bonds: Bonds are debt securities governments, municipalities, or corporations issued to raise capital. When you buy a bond, you lend money to the issuer in exchange for periodic interest payments and the return on the principal investment at maturity. Bonds are generally considered less risky than stocks and can provide steady income, making them a popular choice for conservative investors seeking income generation and capital preservation.

3. Mutual Funds: A mutual fund is a professionally managed investment fund that pools money from multiple investors to invest in a diversified portfolio of stocks, bonds, or other securities. Investing in a mutual fund gives investors instant diversification and access to various assets that may be challenging to attain individually. Mutual funds come in various types, including index funds, actively managed funds, and exchange-traded funds (ETFs), each offering distinct investment strategies and risk profiles.

4. Real Estate Investment Trusts (REITs): REITs are companies that own, operate, or finance income-producing real estate across a range of property sectors such as residential, commercial, and industrial. Investing in REITs provides exposure to the real estate market without the hassles of property management. REITs offer attractive dividend yields and potential capital appreciation, making them popular for income-oriented

investors seeking real estate exposure in their portfolios.

5. Commodity Investments: Commodities are raw materials or primary agricultural products traded in bulk on commodity exchanges. Investors can gain exposure to commodity prices through various investment vehicles such as commodity futures, exchange-traded funds (ETFs), or commodity-focused mutual funds. Commodities provide diversification benefits and can hedge against inflation and economic uncertainties.

Understanding different investment vehicles' characteristics, risks, and potential returns is essential for building a well-rounded investment portfolio that aligns with your financial goals and risk tolerance. By diversifying your investments across various asset classes, you can mitigate risks and position yourself for long-term financial success.

Retirement Planning Strategies

Developing a solid retirement planning strategy becomes increasingly important as individuals progress through their careers and think about retirement. Setting clear financial goals for retirement is the first step towards ensuring a comfortable and secure future. Retirement planning involves saving money and making wise investment decisions to grow those savings over time.

One key component of retirement planning is choosing suitable investment vehicles to help you reach your goals. 401(k) plans and Individual Retirement Accounts (IRAs) are commonly used retirement savings tools.

A 401(k) plan is a tax-advantaged retirement account sponsored by an employer. Employees can contribute a portion of their pre-tax income to a 401(k) account, which can then be invested in stocks, bonds, and mutual funds. Many employers also offer matching contributions, which can significantly boost retirement savings.

On the other hand, IRAs are individual retirement accounts that anyone with earned income can contribute to. There are different types of IRAs, including Traditional and Roth IRAs, each with tax advantages and eligibility criteria. Compared to employer-sponsored 401

(k) plans, IRAs offer individuals more control over their investments and provide a broader range of investment options.

When developing a retirement planning strategy, it is essential to consider your risk tolerance, investment timeline, and financial goals. Regularly reviewing and adjusting your retirement plan is crucial to ensure you stay on track to reach your retirement objectives. You can build a solid foundation for a financially secure retirement by strategically allocating your savings to the right investment vehicles.

- Investment vehicles for retirement savings (401(k), IRAs, etc.)
    When it comes to retirement planning, selecting the right investment vehicles is crucial for building a secure financial future. Two popular options for retirement savings are 401(k) plans and Individual Retirement Accounts (IRAs).
1. **401(k) Plans:** A 401(k) plan is an employer-sponsored retirement savings account that allows employees to contribute a portion of their pre-tax income toward retirement. One of the

key advantages of a 401(k) is the potential for employer matching contributions, which can significantly boost your retirement savings. These plans offer various investment options, such as mutual funds, stocks, and bonds, allowing you to customize your portfolio based on your risk tolerance and investment goals.

Taking full advantage of any employer matching contributions is important, as this is free money that can accelerate your retirement savings growth. Additionally, 401(k) contributions are made automatically through payroll deductions, making them a convenient and disciplined way to save for retirement.

2. **IRAs:** Individual Retirement Accounts (IRAs) are another valuable tool for retirement savings, offering tax advantages that can help maximize your investment returns. There are two main types of IRAs: Traditional and Roth.

- **Traditional IRAs**: Contributions to a Traditional IRA may be tax-deductible, reducing your taxable income in the contribution year. Your investments grow tax-deferred, meaning you won't pay taxes on earnings until you withdraw the funds in retirement.

- **Roth IRAs**: Roth IRAs offer tax-free growth, meaning you contribute after-tax dollars but can withdraw tax-free contributions and earnings in retirement, provided you meet certain criteria. Roth IRAs are particularly advantageous for individuals expecting to be in a higher tax bracket in retirement.

401(k) plans and IRAs offer valuable tax benefits and can help you build a robust retirement portfolio. When choosing between these retirement savings vehicles, it's important to carefully consider your investment options, contribution limits, and withdrawal rules. By leveraging the benefits of 401(k) plans and IRAs, you can take confident steps toward achieving your retirement goals.

Identification and Categorization of Miscellaneous Expenses

Identifying and categorizing miscellaneous expenses is crucial to managing your budget and maintaining financial stability effectively. Although these expenses may seem small or insignificant individually, they can add up quickly and significantly impact your overall financial well-being.

Miscellaneous expenses encompass many items that do not fall neatly into specific budget categories. These expenses include small purchases, unexpected costs, and irregular expenses that may only occur occasionally. It is important to recognize the significance of these expenses and account for them in your budgeting process.

Keep thorough records of your spending habits to identify and categorize miscellaneous expenses. This can include reviewing bank statements, credit card transactions, and receipts to track where your money is being spent. Look for patterns or trends in your expenses to identify common miscellaneous items that may warrant their category in your budget.

Once you have identified these miscellaneous expenses, categorize them based on their frequency and importance. Determine which expenses are essential and which ones can be classified as discretionary. While some miscellaneous expenses may be necessary for your lifestyle or well-being, others may be non-essential and can be reduced or eliminated to free up funds for more critical financial goals.

In categorizing miscellaneous expenses, consider creating separate budget categories or setting aside a specific allowance for these items. This can help you track and allocate funds for these expenses more effectively, preventing them from derailing your overall budget plan. Additionally, prioritizing these expenses based on their impact and importance can help you make informed decisions about allocating your financial resources.

By identifying and categorizing miscellaneous expenses in your budget, you can better understand your spending habits and make more informed financial decisions. This proactive approach to managing miscellaneous expenses can help you maintain control over your finances, reduce financial stress, and work towards achieving your long-term financial goals.

Strategies for Managing Other Expenses

Implementing strategic approaches that promote financial stability and long-term success is crucial for effectively managing other expenses within a budget. Individuals can enhance their budgeting skills and achieve greater control over their financial well-being by employing specific strategies tailored to address miscellaneous costs.

One key strategy for managing other expenses is regularly tracking and categorizing miscellaneous expenditures. This meticulous record-keeping helps individuals comprehensively understand their spending habits and identify areas for potential cost-cutting or optimization. By categorizing miscellaneous expenses into specific groups, such as entertainment, dining out, or personal care, individuals can pinpoint areas where they may be overspending and develop targeted strategies for better allocation of funds.

Another effective technique for managing other expenses is to implement a system for budgeting and allocating funds for unexpected or irregular costs. By setting aside a designated portion of the budget for miscellaneous expenses, individuals can ensure they have a financial safety net to cover unforeseen or emergency expenses without disrupting their overall financial plan. This proactive approach to budgeting helps minimize financial stress and promotes greater peace of mind when navigating unexpected expenses.

Furthermore, prioritizing and adjusting other expenses based on financial goals and priorities is essential for maintaining a balanced budget. By aligning miscellaneous expenditures with overarching financial objectives, individuals can make informed decisions about where to allocate their funds and ensure that their spending habits support their long-term financial aspirations. This deliberate approach to managing other expenses fosters financial discipline and empowers individuals to make wise financial choices that align with their values and goals.

Incorporating these strategic approaches into budget management promotes effective control over miscellaneous expenses and cultivates a mindset of financial responsibility and empowerment. By implementing these strategies for managing other expenses, individuals can strengthen their financial foundation, enhance their budgeting skills, and ultimately achieve greater financial stability and success.

Importance of Flexibility and Adaptability in Budgeting

Budgeting is a cornerstone of effective financial management in personal finance. However, budget rigidity can sometimes hinder one's ability to navigate unforeseen circumstances and adapt to changing financial needs. This is where the importance of flexibility and adaptability in budgeting comes into play.

Flexibility in budgeting allows individuals to respond to unexpected expenses or income fluctuations without derailing their financial stability. Individuals can create a buffer for emergencies or potential opportunities by building some leeway into their budget. This can help prevent financial stress and provide a sense of security, knowing there is room to maneuver when facing unexpected financial challenges.

Moreover, adaptability in budgeting involves the willingness to adjust and reallocate funds based on changing priorities or goals. Life is dynamic, and financial circumstances can shift over time. Being adaptable in budgeting means being open to reassessing one's financial plan regularly and making necessary adjustments to stay on track toward long-term financial objectives.

To ensure financial success, individuals must cultivate a mindset of flexibility and adaptability in budgeting. This requires a proactive approach to financial planning, a willingness to embrace change, and the ability to prioritize financial goals effectively. By integrating flexibility and adaptability into budgeting practices, individuals can better weather financial storms and seize new opportunities, ultimately paving the way for a more secure and prosperous financial future.

Recap of Key Points on Investing and Retirement

The previous chapter delved into investing and retirement planning, exploring essential concepts and strategies for securing one's financial future. It is crucial to understand that investing is not merely about buying stocks or bonds; it is a disciplined approach to growing one's wealth over time.

One key point highlighted was the importance of asset allocation and diversification in a well-rounded investment portfolio. You can reduce risk and enhance potential returns by spreading your investments across different asset classes. Remember, achieving a balance that aligns with your risk tolerance and financial goals is the goal.

Additionally, we discussed the power of compounding interest and the significance of starting early when saving for retirement. Time is your greatest ally in building wealth, and the sooner you begin investing, the greater your potential for long-term growth. Consistent contributions to retirement accounts, such as

401(k)s or IRAs, can significantly impact your financial security in later years.

Furthermore, we emphasized the importance of staying informed about market trends, adjusting your investment strategy as needed, and seeking guidance from financial advisors or professionals when necessary. A proactive approach to monitoring and managing your investments is key to long-term financial success.

As we progress in our financial journey, remember these key points on investing and retirement planning, setting a solid foundation for a secure and prosperous future.

- Summarize the main concepts and strategies discussed in the previous chapter to refresh the reader's memory. In the previous chapter on Investing and Retirement, we explored fundamental concepts and strategies for securing a stable financial future. Understanding the significance of smart investing and diligent retirement planning in building wealth and achieving financial independence.

We emphasized the importance of diversification in investment portfolios to mitigate risks and maximize returns. By spreading investments across various asset classes, such as stocks, bonds, and real estate, individuals can safeguard their wealth against market fluctuations.

Additionally, the chapter delved into the concept of risk tolerance and the correlation between risk and potential returns. Investors must carefully assess their risk appetite and align their investment choices to balance risk and reward.

Moreover, the discussion highlighted the power of compounding interest in growing wealth over time. By reinvesting earnings and allowing them to compound, investors can harness the exponential growth potential of their investments and accelerate their path to financial security.

The key takeaway from the previous chapter is the importance of informed decision-making, long-term planning, and disciplined execution in achieving financial prosperity. By applying these principles and adopting a strategic approach to investing and retirement planning, readers can pave the way for a secure and prosperous financial future.

Importance of Long-Term Financial Planning:

In the previous chapter, we delved into the critical concepts and strategies of investing and retirement planning. We explored the value of diversification, risk management, and the power of compounding interest in building wealth over time. By reviewing these key points, readers can reinforce their understanding of how to make informed financial decisions and set themselves up for long-term success.

Looking ahead, it is essential to emphasize the importance of setting long-term financial goals and planning for retirement. Establishing clear objectives provides a roadmap for your financial journey, guiding your decisions and ensuring that you stay on track to achieve financial security in the future. By envisioning where you want to be in the long run, you can take the necessary steps today to build a stable and prosperous tomorrow.

Moreover, planning for retirement is a fundamental aspect of long-term financial planning. Retirement may seem distant, but the sooner you start preparing, the better positioned you will be to enjoy a comfortable and fulfilling retirement. By saving and investing strategically, you can create a nest egg that will support you during your golden years and allow you to maintain your desired lifestyle without financial stress.

Incorporating long-term financial planning into your overall financial strategy is essential for securing your financial future. It provides peace of mind, stability, and control over your finances. Setting clear goals, developing a solid plan, and committing to consistent action can pave the way for a prosperous and fulfilling financial future.

- Discuss the significance of setting long-term financial goals and planning for retirement.
  Setting long-term financial goals and planning for retirement are crucial steps in ensuring a secure and comfortable future. By establishing clear objectives and creating a roadmap for achieving them, individuals can take control of their

financial well-being and work towards a stable retirement.

When setting financial goals, it is essential to consider factors such as your desired lifestyle in retirement, estimated expenses, and potential sources of income. This process involves evaluating your current financial situation, projecting future needs, and determining how much you need to save to reach your desired retirement goals.

Planning for retirement early offers numerous benefits, primarily due to the power of compounding interest. The earlier you start saving and investing, the more time your money has to grow and multiply. Compounding allows your earnings to generate additional earnings over time, significantly increasing the value of your investments.

Moreover, starting early protects against unexpected setbacks or changes in financial circumstances. By building a strong financial foundation early on, you can weather economic downturns, navigate unforeseen expenses, and secure your financial future.

In addition to the financial aspect, setting long-term goals and planning for retirement also offers peace of mind and a sense of security. A well-thought-out financial plan can alleviate stress about the future, allowing you to focus on enjoying the present while building towards a stable and fulfilling retirement.

In conclusion, setting long-term financial goals and planning for retirement is a fundamental aspect of financial management. Taking proactive steps to outline your objectives, invest wisely, and prepare for the future can pave the way for a financially secure and rewarding retirement journey.

- Highlight the benefits of starting early and the impact of compounding interest on investments.

  Setting long-term financial goals and planning for retirement are crucial steps in securing a stable financial future. One of the key benefits of starting early on this journey is the significant impact of compounding interest on investments. Compounding interest allows your money to grow exponentially over time, as you earn returns not only on your initial investment but also on the accumulated interest.

By starting to invest early, you give your money more time to compound, increasing the potential growth of your investments. This means that even small contributions made in the early stages can accumulate substantial wealth over the long term.

Additionally, starting early allows you to take advantage of the market's power of time. The longer your investments have to weather market fluctuations, the better positioned they are to ride out any short-term volatility and benefit from overall market growth.

Moreover, starting early instills discipline and regular saving habits, essential for long-term financial success. Consistent contributions to your investments over time, no matter how small initially, can lead to significant wealth accumulation and financial security in the future.

In conclusion, the benefits of starting early and understanding the impact of compounding interest on investments cannot be overstated. By taking action now, you are laying the foundation for a financially secure future and positioning yourself for long-term financial success.

Encouragement for Future Financial Success:

Starting early on your financial planning journey can truly make a significant impact on your long-term success. Investing and saving at a younger age gives you the gift of time – a valuable financial resource. The power of compounding interest cannot be overstated in its ability to grow your wealth over time.

As you embark on this journey towards financial success, staying motivated and focused on your goals is important. Remember that every small step you take today will contribute to a brighter financial future tomorrow. Here are some practical tips to help you stay on track:

1. Set Clear Financial Goals: Define what you want to achieve with your finances, whether saving for a new home, funding your children's education, or retiring comfortably. Having clear goals will give you direction and purpose in your financial planning.

2. Create a Budget and Stick to It: Develop a budget aligning with your financial goals and track your expenses to ensure you stay within your means. Be disciplined in following your budget to avoid unnecessary spending and prioritize saving and investing for your future.

3. Seek Professional Advice: Consult with a financial advisor to help create a personalized financial plan tailored to your objectives and risk tolerance. A professional can offer valuable insights and recommendations to optimize your investment strategy and maximize your returns.

4. Stay Educated and Informed: Stay abreast of financial news, trends, and investment opportunities to make informed decisions about your money. Continuous learning and self-education in financial matters will empower you to make smarter choices and confidently navigate the complex world of finance.

5. Stay Committed and Persistent: Rome wasn't built in a day, and neither is a financial success. Stay committed to your financial goals, remain persistent in your efforts, and be patient with the process. Remember that consistency and dedication are key to achieving long-term financial success.

By following these tips and staying dedicated to your financial journey, you will be well on your way to achieving your financial goals and securing a prosperous future for yourself and your loved ones. Embrace the journey with enthusiasm and determination, and watch as your efforts pave the way to a financially secure and fulfilling life.

- Provide motivational insights and practical tips for readers to take action towards achieving their financial goals.

  In the journey towards achieving financial success, it is essential to arm oneself with motivation and practical tips to propel us forward. Setting financial goals is more than just a task - it is a commitment to our future well-being and security.

One key aspect to remember is the importance of seeking professional financial advice. As experts in the field, financial advisors can provide valuable insights tailored to one's circumstances and goals. Their guidance can help us navigate the complex world of investments, retirement planning, and wealth management, ensuring our financial strategies align with our objectives.

Setting realistic targets is another critical factor in achieving financial success. While it is tempting to aim for lofty goals, it is crucial to be practical and set achievable milestones. We can track our progress and stay motivated by breaking down larger objectives into smaller, manageable tasks.

Staying committed to our financial plans requires discipline and resilience. There may be times when obstacles arise or temptations to stray from our budget present themselves. However, staying focused on our long-term goals and the benefits of financial stability can help us overcome these challenges and stay on track toward success.

In conclusion, motivation, seeking professional advice, setting realistic targets, and maintaining commitment are key to achieving financial goals. Incorporating these principles into our financial planning can pave the way for a secure and prosperous future.

- Offer guidance on seeking professional financial advice, setting realistic targets, and staying committed to their financial plans.
  Seeking professional financial advice is crucial in ensuring that your financial goals align with your long-term aspirations. A qualified financial advisor can help you navigate the complexities of investment options, risk management, and retirement planning. By seeking expert guidance, you can benefit from tailored strategies that maximize your financial potential while minimizing unnecessary risks.

Setting realistic targets is key to establishing a solid foundation for your financial plan. It is essential to assess your current financial situation accurately and establish achievable milestones that align with your long-term objectives. You can track your progress and adjust your strategy to stay on course by breaking down your goals into manageable steps.

Staying committed to your financial plans requires discipline and determination. It is easy to get sidetracked by short-term temptations or market fluctuations, but maintaining a long-term perspective is essential for financial success. Regularly reviewing and revising your financial goals, seeking feedback from your financial advisor, and staying focused on your objectives will help you stay on track and realize your financial aspirations. Consistency and perseverance are key elements in achieving financial security and building a stable financial future.

Financial Planning and Wealth Management Strategies

Financial planning is crucial to managing one's wealth effectively. Setting clear financial goals is the first step toward achieving financial success. You can create a roadmap for your financial journey by identifying your short-term and long-term objectives. Whether you are saving for a major purchase, building an emergency fund, or planning for retirement, having specific goals in mind will guide your decision-making process.

Developing wise savings and investment strategies is essential to achieving these goals. This may involve creating a budget, setting aside a portion of your income for savings and investments, and diversifying your portfolio to manage risk. Investing in assets that align with your risk tolerance and financial objectives can help you grow your wealth over time.

Risk management is another key facet of financial planning. Unexpected events such as job loss, medical emergencies, or natural disasters can significantly impact your financial well-being. Having adequate insurance coverage, such as health insurance, life insurance, and property insurance, can provide a safety net during challenging times.

Furthermore, understanding tax laws and regulations is paramount in optimizing your financial situation. Maximizing deductions and credits can help reduce your tax liability, allowing you to keep more of your hard-earned money. Tax-efficient investing strategies, such as utilizing tax-advantaged accounts like IRAs and 401(k)s, can also help you minimize the taxes owed on your investment gains.

In summary, financial planning and wealth management strategies are essential tools for achieving financial stability and success. By setting clear goals, developing sound saving and investing strategies, managing risk through insurance, and optimizing your tax situation, you can take control of your financial future and work towards building long-term wealth.

Tax Planning and Optimization

Tax planning and optimization are critical aspects of financial management that aim to minimize tax liabilities while maximizing opportunities for tax savings. Understanding tax laws and regulations is essential for individuals and businesses to make informed decisions about their financial affairs. Individuals can strategically manage their finances to achieve long-term financial goals by implementing effective tax planning strategies.

One key aspect of tax planning is maximizing deductions and credits available under the tax code. This involves identifying eligible expenses that can be deducted from taxable income, such as charitable contributions, education expenses, and business-related costs. By taking advantage of available tax deductions, individuals can reduce their taxable income and ultimately lower their tax liability.

Tax-efficient investing strategies are another important consideration in tax planning. Individuals can benefit from tax-deferred growth and potential tax savings by strategically allocating investments in tax-advantaged accounts such as IRAs, 401(k)s, and other retirement vehicles. Additionally, tax-loss harvesting and asset location can help minimize tax consequences and optimize investment returns.

Incorporating tax planning into overall financial planning can help individuals achieve their financial goals while minimizing the impact of taxes on their wealth. Individuals can develop a comprehensive tax plan tailored to their specific circumstances and objectives by working with a qualified tax professional or financial advisor. With careful tax planning and optimization, individuals can enhance their financial well-being and build a solid foundation for long-term wealth accumulation and preservation.

Estate Planning and Wealth Transfer

Estate planning is a critical aspect of a comprehensive financial plan. It ensures that your wealth is transferred smoothly and efficiently to your heirs or beneficiaries upon your passing. It involves creating a plan for the management and distribution of your assets in accordance with your wishes while also considering potential tax implications and minimizing estate taxes where possible.

One of the key components of estate planning is creating a will, which outlines how your assets should be distributed after your death. A will allow you to designate specific beneficiaries for your property and assets and establish guardianship for minor children if necessary. By having a clear and legally binding will in place, you can avoid potential conflicts or misunderstandings among family members regarding the distribution of your estate.

In addition to a will, trusts can play a crucial role in estate planning. Trusts are legal arrangements that allow a third party, known as the trustee, to hold and manage assets on behalf of beneficiaries. Trusts offer several benefits, including bypassing probate, maintaining privacy, and providing ongoing asset management for beneficiaries needing more time to handle large inheritances.

Another important consideration in estate planning is minimizing estate taxes to maximize the wealth transferred to your heirs. Strategies such as gifting assets during your lifetime, establishing irrevocable life insurance trusts, and utilizing estate tax exemptions can help reduce the impact of estate taxes on your estate. Working with a qualified estate planning attorney or financial advisor can help you navigate the complexities of estate tax laws and develop a plan that best protects and preserves your wealth for future generations.

Overall, estate planning is a critical component of a sound financial strategy, ensuring that your assets are distributed according to your wishes and minimizing tax liabilities for your heirs. By taking proactive steps to create a comprehensive estate plan, you can provide peace of mind for yourself and your loved ones, knowing that your legacy will be preserved and protected for future generations.

Budget Planning List

Blog Article - Master Brainstorming List for Budget Planning – Stylin Spirit (stylin-spirit.com)

Housing Costs

Mortgages or rent/lease payments:

Principal

Interest

Homeowners Insurance/renters insurance

Understanding the Components of Housing Costs

When considering whether refinancing is viable, it is crucial to have a comprehensive understanding of the various components that make up housing costs. One of the most significant factors to consider is the mortgage rates, representing the cost of borrowing money. This interest is the amount charged by the bank or lending company for allowing you to use their funds, and it is repaid over a specific period, typically ranging from 15 to 30 years. It might surprise you to learn that the larger the personal loans and the longer the repayment period, the more you pay in interest compared to the asset's actual value.

When applying for a home loan, ensuring that there are no prepayment penalties is essential. Prepayment penalties can restrict your ability to make principal-only payments, which can significantly reduce the overall interest paid on the loan and shorten its duration. An excellent strategy to consider is to make an extra monthly payment on your mortgage, as this can help you save a substantial amount of money in the long run, a key aspect of effective debt repayment.

A commonly used rule of thumb is that refinancing may be worthwhile if you can lower the mortgage rates on your home loan by at least 1%. However, it is important to note that if you are currently facing cash flow issues, extending the personal loan period may provide temporary relief, although it will ultimately increase the overall cost of financing over the loan's lifetime.

Home insurance is another important aspect to consider regarding housing costs. The cost of homeowners insurance is influenced by several factors, including deductibles, liability coverage, supplemental coverage for valuable items such as art or jewelry, and the expenses associated with rebuilding in the event of loss or damage. Reviewing and updating these considerations annually is crucial to account for inflation and ensure that you are adequately protected and not underinsured.

For those who rent or lease their residence, it is equally important to carefully review the rental or lease agreement to ensure that your home insurance coverage adequately protects you from potential losses. It is worth noting that the homeowner's insurance policy of the property owner typically only covers your personal possessions if explicitly stated in your agreement.

By understanding the various components of housing costs, such as mortgage rates, prepayment penalties, and home insurance coverage, you can make informed decisions about refinancing and ensure you are adequately protected financially. Reviewing and updating these factors regularly, including the terms of your personal loans, will help you stay on top of your housing costs and make the most financially sound choices for your situation.

Home equity loans or line of credit payments

Homeowners Association Dues

Sewer

Water

Landscaping maintenance

The cost of landscaping can fluctuate significantly throughout the year, depending on the climate of the area you live in. This is an important consideration when planning your landscaping project. Factors such as seasonal changes, weather conditions, and the specific needs of the plants and materials you choose can influence the expenses associated with maintaining and beautifying your outdoor space. For instance, in regions with harsh winters, you may need to invest in winterizing your garden or protecting delicate plants from frost damage. Conversely, in areas with hot and dry summers, considerations like irrigation systems or drought-resistant plants might be necessary to ensure the longevity and vitality of your landscape. By comprehending the impact of climate on landscaping costs, you can make informed decisions and create a beautiful outdoor space that thrives in your specific environment.

Pest control

Natural Gas

Propane (for rural homes)

Electricity

Cable, satellite, dish, streaming, or other subscription costs

Internet

Phone (Landline and or cell phone)

Utility providers often raise their rates periodically, influenced by long-term trends and seasonal fluctuations. If managing your monthly expenses is a concern, opting for level payments throughout the year is beneficial. Many utility companies offer this option, but you can also independently implement this strategy to manage your fixed expenses. For example, in regions with warmer climates, the cost of air conditioning tends to rise sharply during the summer months. By spreading your payments evenly over the year, you can better anticipate and manage these increased expenses, ensuring a more stable financial situation.

Home Maintenance

A home repair fund (for the breakdown of equipment)

Understanding the age of your appliances, air conditioning, and furnace can provide valuable information for your savings and investment accounts. This knowledge lets you anticipate when they might require maintenance or replacement, helping you plan and budget accordingly. Furthermore, it can help you make informed decisions about energy efficiency. Older appliances and HVAC systems are often less energy-efficient than newer models, leading to higher utility bills. By knowing the age of these items, you can assess whether investing in newer, more energy-efficient alternatives is more cost-effective. This knowledge empowers you to maintain the functionality and efficiency of your household appliances, air conditioning, and furnace, saving you time, money, and potential headaches in the long run.

Home maintenance (annual furnace tune-up, lawn care, gardening, etc.)

A home upgrade/remodel fund (new appliances, painting needs, etc.)

A new furniture fund

Tax preparation and legal fees

Vehicle and Transportation Costs

Vehicle purchase payments or lease payments

Auto insurance premiums

Insurance deductibles

Fuel costs

Public transportation

Parking expenses

A vehicle maintenance fund (oil changes, car washes, new tires, wiper fluid, etc.)

Toll fees

Vehicle registration and DMV costs

A vehicle repair fund (to fund future vehicle repair costs)

Vehicle storage costs

Transportation costs specific to your commute

Parking fees

Groceries & Household Supplies

General groceries and cleaning supplies

Social/family gatherings

Holiday food funds

Eating out (including lunch for work)

First-aid supplies

Vitamins and other health supplements

Non-prescription (over-the-counter) medicines

Haircare products

Employment Related Expenses

Work clothing/uniforms

Dry cleaning expenses

Client gifts and other client expenses

Professional fees

Licensing costs (if applicable)

Continuing education costs

Work travel expenses

Coworker gifts and celebration-related expenses

Work-related social gatherings

Health and Medical

A clinic and hospital copay fund

Prescription medicines

Dental care costs

Eye care costs

Naturopathic, homeopathic, and alternative health costs

Medical equipment

Orthodontic care

Out-of-pocket deductibles

Health insurance premiums

HSA and FSA contributions

New baby/child medical expenses

Annual Checkups and Copays

Personal Care

Clothing purchases

Haircuts and other salon services

Beauty products such as makeup and fragrances

Athletic gear like running shoes

Health club membership fees

Fun money (for friends and other miscellaneous gatherings)

Self-care activity money (anything you do to rejuvenate and refresh)

Hobby expenses

Children and Dependents

Childcare expenses (daycare and babysitters/nannies)

Clothing

Haircuts and other grooming costs

School supplies

School lunches

Sports and extracurricular activities

Summer camps

Toys and learning activities

Miscellaneous social/friend outings

Baby formula, diapers, and other baby costs

Allowances

Pet Care

Pet purchase fund

Pet food

Annual vet costs (check-ups, vaccinations, dewormer, etc.)

Emergency vet costs

Pet insurance (if applicable)

Training costs (if applicable)

Pet boarding/pet care costs

Grooming costs

City/county pet license costs

Other pet supplies (toys, leashes, litter supplies, etc.)

Holiday, Family, and Religion

Tithing to your local church or other religious organization

Charitable donations to causes you support

Birthday gifts

Anniversary gifts

Wedding gifts

Graduation gifts

Holiday gifts such as Easter, Christmas or Hanukkah

Bar Mitzvah, baptism, or other religious celebration gifts

Giving to your community

Social and Entertainment

Theatre, opera, and other shows

Music concerts

Day trips

Museum and Historical Society membership dues

Camping, hiking, and other nature excursions

Holiday events

Family gatherings and events

Summer gatherings such as BBQs

Friend gatherings

Sporting events (viewing)

Participatory sporting events (marathons, fun runs)

Weekend getaways

Summer vacations

Winter vacations

Debt Service other than Mortgage

Student loan payments

Credit card payments

Knowing your credit score and monitoring credit card promotions is beneficial as it informs you about various options. By staying updated with the market, you may find opportunities to transfer your outstanding balance to a different lender offering a more reasonable interest rate. Some lenders may even offer promotional introductory periods with zero percent interest options, which can be highly beneficial for credit consolidation. Considering home equity loans to reduce your interest expenses might be worthwhile if you have significant credit card debt. However, maintaining healthy spending habits is crucial to protect yourself against overwhelming debt. While unavoidable emergencies can occur, being financially responsible can help mitigate their impact.

Auto loan payments

Other personal loan payments

Repayment of loans from family

Loans for recreational vehicles

Insurance

Term Life Insurance

Auto Insurance

Health Insurance

Income Protection Insurance

Long-Term Disability Insurance

Long-Term Care Insurance (if you're age 60 or older)

Identity Theft Insurance

Business Insurance

Umbrella Policy (if you have a net worth of $500,000 or more)

Investing and Retirement

Emergency fund savings

401k savings

IRA or other retirement savings

Non-retirement investment funds

Transaction fees

Brokerage fees

Other

Upgraded house fund

Replacement car fund

Vacation fund

College savings (for yourself, your children, or your grandchildren)

Financial independence/retire early fund

Other sinking fund purposes

www.ingramcontent.com/pod-product-compliance
Lightning Source LLC
Chambersburg PA
CBHW052255220526
45471CB00001B/347